ON BECOMING A
MATURE CHRISTIAN

*How to experience consistent victory
in the Christian life*

DAMIAN CHAMBERS

First Printing: 2019

ISBN 9781723793523

I dedicate this book to all who are striving to make heaven their home and to form a character after the likeness of Christ.

Contents

Foreword 8

Introduction 9

CHAPTER 1 Why We Need to Grow 10

Why is growing up important?.. 11

We were planted to bear fruit 12

What doesn't grow is either dying or dead 12

Growing up is a great blessing.. 13

CHAPTER 2 What is Spiritual Maturity?....................15

The Babe in Christ 15

The Mature in Christ.. 16

How do I know if I am mature? 16

Character and Maturity... 17

Faith and Maturity 17

Understanding of the Truth and Maturity 18

Spiritual Babes vs. Spiritually Mature...................................... 18

CHAPTER 3 Maturity in Love 21

Love is patient ("charity *suffereth long*") 25

Love is self-sacrificial ("charity . . . is *kind*") 26

Love celebrates the good in others ("charity *envieth* not") 28

Love does not boast ("charity *vaunteth not* itself") 28

Love is not proud ("charity. . . is *not puffed up*").................... 29

Love is not rude ("charity . . . doth not behave itself *unseemly*")
.... 29

Love is not selfish ("charity . . . *seeketh not her own*")........... 30

Love is not boisterous (charity . . . *is not easily provoked*") 31

Love keeps no record of wrongs ("charity . . . *thinketh no evil*")
.... 32

Love endures all things ("charity . . . *endureth* all things")....... 33

CHAPTER 4 Maturity in Faith 36

Faith accepts that God is 39

Faith accepts who God is 40

God is everywhere you need Him................................... 41

God knows everything... 43

God can do all that He promises 46

God is faithful 47

God loves us unconditionally 48

Faith Accepts our obligation to obey God 49

CHAPTER 5 Maturity in Understanding 50

The Nature of Man 52

The Great Controversy.. 55

The Life, Death and Resurrection of Christ 58

The Experience of Salvation 59

Christ's Ministry in the Heavenly Sanctuary.................. 61

CHAPTER 6 How We Become Mature.....................65

The Word of God provides the resources for growth 66

Read it every day...67

Study it diligently..68

Observation:...69

Interpretation:..69

Application: 70

Memorize it 70

Obey its principles 71

The Holy Spirit keeps us alive Spiritually 72

Prayer Keeps us Connected 73

Why pray when God already knows? 74

What are some of the things we should pray for? 75

Guidelines for effective prayer 75

Set aside specific time and place to pray. 75

Exercise faith 76

Penitence 76

Forgiveness 76

Do not cherish any known sins 77

Perseverance in Prayer 77

Definiteness 77

Plan what you are going to pray about 78

Develop and use various patterns of prayer 78

Don't become a hermit 78

Maintain an attitude of thanksgiving and praise to God ... 78

Trials keep us humble 79

Understanding Trials 80

Trials are part of God's plan to help us grow 81

Trials evoke the deepest emotions and inspirations 81

Trials prepare us to help others 82

We will never face a trial that is beyond our ability to endure .. 82

We may have to live with some trials all our lives 83

We can lose the blessing of trials 83

How to Overcome Trials 84

Be prepared 84

Keep the connection line 84

Take notes 84

Do not give up on God even if you make mistakes 84

Praise and Thanksgiving 85

Keep the end in mind 85

Temptation keeps us vigilant 86

Do not become *discouraged* or *frightened* by temptation. 86

Maintain a constant devotional life. 86

Recognize the vulnerable situations and circumstances 87

Seek God's help 87

Recognize that there is always *a way out* (1 Corinthians 10:13). ...88

Refocus your attention on godly thoughts...................................88

Realize your vulnerability 88

Witnessing keeps us on the cutting edge 89

Steps to becoming an effective witness for Christ........................90

Be converted 90

Know your area of giftedness 90

Know the Bible 90

Seek training...91

Use Christ's Method of Witnessing.....................................91

Start witnessing to those next to you 92

Utilize the power of prayer in our witnessing.........................92

Possess a meek spirit...93

Growing together 93

Mentorship 95

Support...96

Conclusion 96

CHAPTER 7 Hindrances to Spiritual Growth............98

"No Deepness of Earth" 99

Neglect of devotional exercises..101

Unwillingness to surrender to the word....................................102

Lack of nurture or discipleship..102

"The Thorns"... 102

Cherished Sins 103

Worldly ambitions 105

Conclusion..108

About the Author..110

Foreword

On Becoming a Mature Christian – "How to experience consistent victory in the Christian Life," advances timeless gems of truth that are relevant for every human being, not just committed Christians. However, to those who have already intentionally embarked upon the journey to the kingdom, it provides motivation, inspiration, and challenge.

The real-life illustrations from farming to traveling and others that are employed embed the timeless scriptural principles in readers' minds that make them not soon forgotten. This book does not only present ideas, concepts and principles, but it is also like a "how to guide." It tells Kingdom aspirants what to do to mature in Christ. The wisely adopted biblical mantras and practical life stories are value added that enhances its applicability and relevance.

Not only do I endorse the content of this book, but I also congratulate Pastor Damian Chambers for the empowered and spiritually fertile mind that produces it. Christian growth and development at this stage of the journey is boosted – read, practice and share it!

Dr. Balvin B. Braham
Administrative Field Secretary
Assistant to the President; Evangelism and Leadership Development
Inter-American Division of Seventh-day Adventists

Introduction

One of my greatest fear as a young Christian was the fear of failure. I was not worried about not doing well; I was afraid of doing well, then end up failing. What do I mean? When I reflected on the lives of some great men in the Bible like King Solomon, the wisest man who ever lived, who despite his brilliant beginnings, he ended up straying from the right path (at least for a while). Outside of the Bible, many did great things for the Lord; yet for some reason or another, they end up losing out on eternal life.

I asked myself, "if these men were so brilliant and had such privileges; yet they failed, what about me?" What will it take to have success in the Christian life? As I grew in understanding, I recognized, that, in the Christian walk, success is not necessarily great success, but consistent success. I realized that our focus should not be on our progress and abilities; our focus should be on Christ and what He can do for us. Therefore, I realized that complete and consistent dependence on God is our only hope of success in this walk. I discovered that our biggest problem is not that we do not know the secret to success; we neglect to keep doing what is required.

In this book, I present a formula for maintaining a consistent connection with Jesus—Christian Maturity. Christian Maturity is about knowing how to keep going despite the challenges and distractions in the way.

CHAPTER 1
Why We Need to Grow

Have you ever done any farming? That is something we loved to do as children while growing up in rural Jamaica. We enjoyed planting seeds and sometimes a few yam heads. With anxiety and excitement, we watched the sprouts blossomed. For us, they took too long to grow as we watched every day for signs of growth.

Interestingly, I cannot remember ever reaping anything from our farming as children. The truth is, it did not matter to us. What mattered was that we loved to watch plants grow. For us, farming was a mere hobby.

A real farmer cannot farm like this. A farmer whose livelihood depends on results, takes a different approach—the object of his farming is harvesting; not just to watch plants grow.

So, it is with the Christian life. There are persons whose Christian experience are like us children who farmed for fun—they get baptized, regularly attend Church, read the Bible and pray, yet their Christian life is fruitless. They do not have a definite aim for their Christian life, except maybe to make sure that they go to Church every week.

Like the real farmer, who expects to have a harvest, God expects all Christians to bear fruit. The Bible refers to each new Christian as being 'born again' or 'the planting of the Lord' (John 3:3, 5, 6; Isaiah 61:3). And like the farmer who plants and nurtures his crop so that he can reap, God's desire for every Christian is that they grow up in Him to be mature, fruit-bearing sons and daughters of God. The fruit, here, represents the reproduction of Christ's character in the life of the Christian.

According to Ellen G. White, "Christ is seeking to reproduce Himself in the hearts of men; and He does this through those who believe in Him. The object of the Christian life is fruit bearing—the reproduction of Christ's character in the believer, that it may be reproduced in others."[1] According to the Apostle Paul in Romans 8:29, "For whom he did foreknow, he also did predestinate [to be] conformed to the image of his Son, that he might be the firstborn among many brethren."

The goal of the Christian life, the finished product, is to be like Jesus. The Apostle John also noted in 1 John 3:2, 3, "Beloved, now are we the sons of God, and it doth not yet appear what we shall be: but we know that, when he shall appear, we shall be like him; for we shall see him as he is. And every man that hath this hope in him purifieth himself, even as he is pure."

Why is growing up important?

The Christian life is not easy. Without a clear understanding of our goal as Christians, the Christian experience will appear to be an endless array of difficulties, trials, and temptations. With such an outlook, some easily welcome discouragement and self-pity. In the face of discouragement, some persons respond by doing one of the following:

1. give up on their Christian life (**backslide**) [2 Peter 2:20-22; Hebrews 10:35);

2. settle for a mediocre experience (**compromise**); [Revelation

3:14-17] or

3. or establish their standards of Christian perfection [Galatians 3:1-3; Romans 10:1-3] (*legalism*).

All three positions are dangerous.

We were planted to bear fruit

We have already highlighted one of the main reasons it is important for us to grow—we are to bear fruit—this is the object of the Christian life. This point is made clear in the parable of the vineyard in Isaiah 5:1-7. God, in the parable, represents His people as a vineyard that He has planted, expecting it to bring forth grapes, but instead, it brought forth wild grapes (Isaiah 5:2). God expresses disappointment with the fact that He did all He could for the vineyard—in that He built a tower and a winepress in it, fenced it, and gathered out the stones—yet the vineyard brought forth wild grapes. "What could have been done more to my vineyard, that I have not done in it," the Lord exclaims (Isaiah 5:4). So, it is that God is disappointed when we do not bear the fruit He is expecting us to bear as Christians.

What doesn't grow is either dying or dead

Secondly, it is very important for us to grow, because whatever is not growing is either dying or dead. According to John the Baptist, "…the ax is laid unto the root of the trees: therefore, every tree which bringeth not forth good fruit is hewn down and cast into the fire" (Matthew 3:10). Jesus also said, "I am the true vine, and my Father is the husbandman. Every branch in me that beareth not fruit he taketh away: . . . If a man abides not in me, he is cast forth as a branch, and is withered; and men gather them, and cast [them] into the fire, and they are burned" (John 15:1-6). Therefore, a Christian who fails to grow faces the prospect of losing out on eternal life. There is no space for mediocre in God's book

(Revelation 3:14-21).

God wants His people not only to be planted or to show signs of growth but to become mature. In the parable of the "Sower who went forth to sow," Jesus taught that only the seeds that fell on "good ground" and brought forth fruit gave glory to God. The other seeds which fell on 'stony' and 'thorny' soils showed signs of growth, but they never brought forth any fruit (Matthew 13:1-23). These 'sprouts' represent Christians who start the journey and fail to continue to the end or fail to grow up.

According to Ellen G. White,

"There are those who attempt to ascend the ladder of Christian progress; but as they advance they begin to put their trust in the power of man, and soon lose sight of Jesus, the Author, and Finisher of their faith. The result is failure--the loss of all that has been gained. Sad indeed is the condition of those who, becoming weary of the way, allow the enemy of souls to rob them of the Christian graces that have been developing in their hearts and lives."[2]

Growing up is a great blessing

Finally, we should not only see it as a duty to grow up in Christ but also a privilege. Christian maturity is the "prize of the high calling of God," which every Christian should press towards (Philippians 3:14). The fact that God calls us to it means that He has made provision for us to make it. "According as his divine power hath given unto us all things that [pertain] unto life and godliness, through the knowledge of him that hath called us to glory and virtue: Whereby are given unto us exceeding great and precious promises: that by these ye might be partakers of the divine nature, having escaped the corruption that is in the world through lust." (2 Peter 1:3, 4). It was on this basis that Peter urged the brethren not to settle for mediocrity, but to "add to their faith" and to "grow in grace, and [in] the knowledge of our Lord and Saviour Jesus Christ" (2 Peter 3:18).

According to the Apostle John, "Herein is our love made perfect (mature), that we may have boldness in the day of judgment: because as he is, so are we in this world. There is no fear in love; but perfect love casteth out fear: because fear hath torment. He that feareth is not made perfect in love" (1 John 4:17, 18 margins).

---

[1] Ellen G. White, *Christ Object Lessons* (Silver Spring, Maryland: Better Living Publications, 1990), 67.

[2] Ellen G. White, *Acts of the Apostles* (Miami, Florida: Inter-American Division Publishing Association, 1911), 532-533.

CHAPTER 2
What is Spiritual Maturity?

Most of us can remember the first time we attempted to ride a bicycle. We listened attentively to the instructions of our teacher/coach. We watched as he or she demonstrates. However, when it's our turn, we did not do so well at balancing as we thought we should. It took some time for us, after much practice, to get over the awkwardness of trying to keep our balance while focusing on where we are going.

For a new Christian, getting adjusted to keeping their focus on Jesus all the time can be challenging. We often get distracted and forget where we are going. Maturity in Christ represents practicing constant and consistent dependence on the Lord.

In this chapter, we will look at what the Bible teaches about spiritual maturity.

The Babe in Christ

The word that is translated as "babes" in the New Testament is the Greek word *nepios*. *Nepios* is derived from a combination of two other Greek words, *ne* (which means "not") and *epo* (which means "to speak"). From this word is derived the meaning, "an infant, a child not yet able to speak plainly" or "a babe in Christ, a person weak in faith."[1] This word refers to Christians who are young in the faith and are still learning the basic principles of Christianity. "Babes" can also be used to refer to Christians who are not so young (regarding the length of time they have been Christians), but who have not yet perfected the grace of the Spirit in their lives (Hebrews 5:12-14).

The Mature in Christ

On the other hand, the mature ("full of age") are those who are referred to in the King James Version of the Bible as being "perfect." The word perfect (in this context), comes from a Greek word (*telos*) which means "adult, fully-grown, or full of age."[2] The term 'perfect' here doesn't necessarily refer to one who is without fault, but, one who is mature in faith[3]. The word refers to "a stage of spiritual maturity that marks those who are steadfast in the faith under all circumstances."[4]

How do I know if I am mature?

The Bible identifies three areas for measuring maturity--our character (behavior); our faith (beliefs), and our understanding (knowledge) of truth. Character is the result of God's Work in us; faith is how we enter and maintain a relationship with God and understanding is our knowledge of the truths that fuel or give the reason for our faith.

In the following section, I will examine what the Bible teaches about spiritual maturity by comparing the mature and the babe under the general headings of love, faith, and understanding. All three dimensions speak to how we relate to the truth (the Word of God). Love demonstrates how we practice the truth; faith refers to our belief of the truth and understanding, how much we know the truth. It takes all three to measure maturity. If we, for example, measure maturity merely by how much we know the truth, we will be misguided.

Character and Maturity

According to the Bible, Christian maturity is measured by our behavior (character). The Apostle Paul attributed immature spiritual behavior as the reason for the divisiveness that existed among the Corinthians. He said, ". . . I, brethren, could not speak unto you as unto spiritual, but as unto carnal, even as unto babes in Christ. I have fed you with milk, and not with meat: for hitherto ye were not able to bear it, neither yet now are ye able. For ye are yet carnal: for whereas there is among you envying, and strife, and divisions, are ye not carnal, and walk as men?" (1 Corinthians 3:1–3). On the other hand, the mature Christian practices unconditional love towards others (1 Corinthians 13:4-8).

The author of Hebrews laments that the believers, who should have been mature Christians long ago, were still in need of being taught the basic doctrine of repentance towards God and others. This suggests that they were not as consistent in their walk with God as they should be. The author refers to them as babes.

Faith and Maturity

The Bible also speaks to maturity in faith. The Apostle John declares, "Herein is our love made perfect (mature), that we may have boldness in the day of judgment: because as he is, so are we in this world. There is no fear in love; but perfect love casteth out fear: because fear hath torment. He that feareth is not made perfect in love" (1 John 4:17-18). Immaturity in faith is demonstrated by one who is troubled with uncertainty about the future of their Christian life and the things of God. Therefore, these persons will have trouble taking on a positive outlook when trials come. They will see trials as punishment. On the other hand, the mature Christian would have proven by experience that God's word cannot fail.

Understanding of the Truth and Maturity

According to the Bible, maturity is also measured by our level of understanding of the truth. The Apostle Paul told the Ephesian believers that those who are still "tossed to and fro" in their minds about the truth are children and are not yet mature (Ephesians 4:14-15). That is why the babes in Christ ought to be fed with milk and not with strong meat. They are to feed on the basic principles of the word of God until they are established in the faith (1 Peter 2:1-2 and Hebrews 5:13-15). On the other hand, the mature knows what truth is and are not easily led astray by error.

Spiritual Babes vs. Spiritually Mature

Table 1: Comparing the mature in character/behavior to the babe.

The Babe in Character	The Mature in Character
Struggles with envy and strife (1 Corinthians 3:1-3).	Practices maturity in love (1 Corinthians 13:4-8; Matthew 5:38-48).
Obeys God to merit His favor (Matthew 5:20; Luke 18:9-14).	Obeys God because he loves God and knows that life and true happiness can only be preserved by doing so (1 John 5:3).
Must be coerced and scolded into obedience. i.e. *the children of Israel in the wilderness experience*	Needs only to be told what to do. i.e. *Caleb and Joshua*

Continually stumbles and need again and again to be taught the doctrine of repentance towards God and assurance of salvation (Hebrews 5:12).	Daily walks by faith in obedience to God's word; if he or she makes mistakes, he or she confesses and repents immediately and continues to follow the Lord (Philippians 3:12-14).

Table 2: Comparing the child in faith to the mature in faith

The Child in Faith	*The Mature in Faith*
Gets discouraged and complains about trials and temptations.	Accepts trials as a normal part of his/her experience and uses them as opportunities to grow.
Sees chastening as a sign of God's displeasure (Hebrews 12:3-12).	Accepts God's chastening as a sign of love.
Troubled with uncertainty and fear about the future (1 John 4:17, 18).	Understands that one's future and success as a Christian is based upon God's will united with his/her choices to obey God.

Table 3: Comparing the mature in understanding to the babe in understanding

The Babe in Understanding	The Mature in Understanding
Tossed to and fro in his/her mind about the truth (Ephesians 4:14-15).	Knows what he or she believes and has proven truth by study and experience (Hebrews 5:14).
Feeds on milk (1 Peter 2:2; Heb. 5:13).	Feeds on strong meat (Hebrews 5:13, 14).

In the next three chapters, we will expound on the three areas of the Christian life by which we measure spiritual maturity--*love, faith, and understanding.*

---

[1] Spiros Zodhates, *Lexical Aids to the New Testament, Revised Edition* (Chattanooga: AMG Publishers, 1991), 1740.

[2] Ibid, 1761-62.

[3] Ibid, 1761.

[4] "Biblical Research Institute", Edward Heppenstall, accessed September 26, 2018, https://adventistbiblicalresearch.org/sites/default/files/pdf/perfection%20Heppenstall.pdf.

CHAPTER 3
Maturity in Love

Love is the fruit (result) of God's Work in us.

God is the source of love (John 4:7-8). Love is not only the way God operates, but it is also how He expects to maintain peace and happiness among His subjects. The principles of love are outlined in the Ten Commandments and are founded on two principles—love for God and love for our fellowmen (Matthew 22:37-40).

Love calls us to think, speak and act based on *reverence* for God and *respect* for our fellow men. The first four of the Ten Commandments call us to put God first in our lives, worship Him only, respect His holy Name and His Holy Day. The last six Commandments call us to respect human authority (especially our parents), have sacred regard for human life, be sexually pure, respect the property of others, be true and honest, and avoid covetousness (see Exodus 20:3-17). If all men operated by the principles of love, there would be no war, unhappiness or hatred in the world.

However, sin produced in man's heart rebellion against God and hatred for each other. The Bible describes the condition of the heart of fallen man as being at "enmity against God: for it is not subject to the law of God, neither indeed can be. So then", the

Apostle Paul concludes, "they that are in the flesh cannot please God" (Romans 8:7, 8).

In that condition, the works that are manifested in man's life are, "....Adultery, fornication, uncleanness, lasciviousness, Idolatry, witchcraft, hatred, variance, emulations, wrath, strife, seditions, heresies, envyings, murders, drunkenness, revellings" -- everything that is contrary to the loving principles of God's Commandments (Galatians 5:19-21).

Nevertheless, through the atoning sacrifice of Jesus and the work of the Holy Spirit in our hearts, God breaks down selfishness and begin the work of restoring the principles of love in our lives. According to the Apostle Paul, this work bears its fruit in ". . . . Love, joy, peace, longsuffering, gentleness, goodness, faith, meekness, temperance:" (Galatians 5:22, 23). Love is the "good work" that God begins to produce in us when we accept Him and which He will continue until the day of Jesus Christ (Philippians 1:6).

That is why our development as Christians ought to be measured by love. Here is what Jesus referred to when He said, "Be ye therefore perfect, even as your Father which is in heaven is perfect" (Matthew 5:48). The context of Matthew chapter 5 presents Jesus calling us to be mature in our love for others, just as our heavenly Father is. Mature love is unconditional and unselfish -- it considers the welfare of others above itself, including its enemies (Matthew 5:38-48).

Therefore, the moral goal that God has for His children is to be made perfect in love. To be "merciful, as your Father also is merciful . . . [who] "is kind unto the unthankful and to the evil" (Luke 6:36, 35 margins). "By this shall all [men] know that ye are my disciples" Jesus said, "if ye have love one to another" (John 13:35).

This unconditional love, which comes from the Greek word 'agape', is also translated in the *King James Version* of the Bible as 'charity'. In the Apostle Peter's 'ladder of Christian growth', charity is placed at the top end of the ladder (as illustrated in figure 1.1), clearly saying that love (charity) is the destination mark in character development for the Christian.

"And beside this, giving all diligence, add to your faith virtue; and to virtue knowledge; and to knowledge temperance; and to temperance patience; and to patience godliness; And to godliness brotherly kindness; and to brotherly kindness charity" (2 Peter 1:5-7).

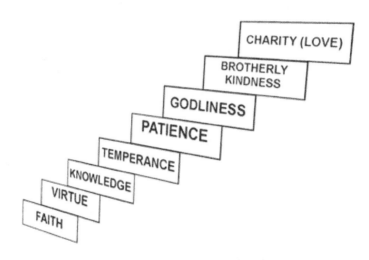

Figure 1: Ladder of Christian growth based on 2 Peter 1

Paul also declared love as the goal of the Christian's character-building process. He says without 'charity' (love) nothing else adds up.

"Though I speak with the tongues of men and of angels, but have not love, I have become sounding brass or a clanging cymbal. And though I have *the gift of* prophecy, and understand all mysteries and all knowledge, and though I have all faith, so that I could remove mountains, but have not love, I am nothing. And though I bestow all my goods to feed *the poor*, and though I give my body to be burned, but have not love, it profits me nothing" (1 Corinthians 13:1-3, NKJV).

The Apostle Paul told the Corinthian believers that despite their spiritual gifts such as speaking in tongues, prophesying, healing or faith if they did not have love, they were not progressing in the Christian walk.

Earlier in the Chapter, Paul told the believers that selfishness, envying and divisions among them was as a sign that they were making little progress.

"And I, brethren," the Apostle Paul said to them, "could not speak to you as to spiritual *people* but as to carnal, as to babes in Christ. I fed you with milk and not with solid food; for until now you were not able *to receive it*, and even now you are still not able; for you are still carnal. For where *there are* envy, strife, and divisions among you, are you not carnal and behaving like *mere* men?" (1 Corinthians 3:1-3, NKJV).

The goal of the Christian's character development is to love as Christ loves. It is so easy to get side-tracked concerning the goal of the Christian life. Some persons measure their growth by the amount of time they spend in prayer, studying the Bible or attending Church, others by the number of sermons they preach and whether they can speak in tongues. But for Jesus the yardstick of our character development is LOVE.

To get a clearer understanding of what love is, I'll share the Apostle Paul's definition from the New King James Version with brief comments:-
1 Corinthians 13:4-8,
"Love suffers long
and is kind;
love does not envy;
love does not parade itself,
is not puffed up;
does not behave rudely,
does not seek its own,
is not provoked,
thinks no evil;

does not rejoice in iniquity,
but rejoices in the truth;
bears all things,
believes all things,
hopes all things,
endures all things."

Love is patient ("charity suffereth long")

The Greek word translated as "suffers long," is *makrothumeou* which means "to be long-suffering," as opposed to being given to hasty anger or punishment. It involves exercising understanding and patience both towards God (James 5:7, 8) and persons (Matthew 18:26, 29). It is the same word used by the Apostle Peter to define God's attitude towards the sinner, "The Lord is not slack concerning his promise, as some men count slackness; but is *longsuffering* to us-ward, not willing that any should perish, but that all should come to repentance" (2 Peter 3:9 *emphasis supplied*).

When used in this context, of God's attitude towards us, the word long-suffering explains what led God to delay His punishment of the sinner to give an opportunity for the sinner to repent. Therefore, it has to do with being forgiving; overlooking one's faults while seeking an opportunity for reconciliation. For God to be long-suffering towards us, it cost Him the life of His Son; for God is both just and merciful. Therefore, being merciful, He forgave our sins; being just He gave His Son to suffer the penalty of sin on our behalf (Isaiah 53:6, 7; 2 Corinthians 5:21; Romans 8:31-34).

God invites us to share with Him this attribute of being long-suffering, forgiving, merciful and patient. Because God is unconditionally long-suffering towards us, He calls us to do the same for others. We are not called to pay for the sins of those who offend us, for this we could not do. All that God is asking us to do is to be as long-suffering towards others as He has been towards us. One very important sign of spiritual immaturity is when Christians are not willing to exercise forbearance towards each other or even towards God (1 Corinthians 3:1-3).

Jesus also gave a parable to teach how unreasonable it is for us not to forgive as God has forgiven us. The parable is about a king who was taking account of his servants. Upon doing so, the king found a servant who owed him 10,000 talents. The King was about to give a command for the servant, his wife, and children to be sold into slavery to recover his money. However, the servant begged the King, "Lord, have patience (*makrothumeou*) with me....." The King's had compassion on him and he forgave the servant his debt. However, it so happened that this servant (who the king forgave him his debt of 10,000 talents) went out and found a fellow servant who owed him 100 pence. Instead of exercising mercy towards the fellow servant, this servant demanded that his fellow servant should pay; even after the fellow servant begged him, "have patience (*makrothumeou*) with me....." The other servants who witnessed what happened went and told the king how cruel the forgiven servant was, and the king was so angry that he withdrew his kindness from the wicked servant.

"So likewise," Jesus concluded, "shall my heavenly Father do also unto you, if ye from your hearts forgive not everyone his brother their trespasses" (Matthew 18:23-35).

Love is self-sacrificial ("charity . . . is kind")

The word here translated as kind is the Greek word, "*Krestos*," which is synonymous to "goodness," "gracious" and means, "to furnish what is needed." Therefore, kindness goes along with giving. However, this word goes further than giving, for it does not only mean to give to those we love, but to give because someone is in need. In other words, kindness does not consider the worthiness of the recipient, but their need. This is the type of kindness that led the Samaritan man to stop and help the wounded Jew (see Luke 10:25-37). The Samaritan did not consider the social status or class of the man in need, but the very fact that he needed help was reason enough to help him. According to George R. Knight, in his book, My Gripe with God, "normal people give others what they deserve, but . . . . God gives them what they need."[1]

We can conclude, therefore, that it was kindness that led God to give His only Begotten Son as an atoning sacrifice for our sins, not because we are worthy of it, but because we needed it (John 3:16). Kindness is thus synonymous with 'grace' -- God's unmerited favor towards the sinner.

Kindness is an attribute God wants us to share. As much as He is kind towards us, He wants us to be kind to others. The Apostle Paul, writing to the young preacher Titus, asked him to warn the brethren, to ". . . . speak evil of no man, to be no brawlers, but gentle, shewing all meekness unto all men. For we ourselves also were sometimes foolish, disobedient, deceived, serving divers lusts and pleasures, living in malice and envy, hateful, and hating one another. But after that the kindness and love of God our Saviour toward man appeared, Not by works of righteousness which we have done, but according to his mercy he saved us, by the washing of regeneration, and renewing of the Holy Ghost;" (Titus 3:2-5).

To the brethren in Ephesus, Paul wrote, "Let all bitterness, and wrath, and anger, and clamour, and evil speaking, be put away from you, with all malice: And be ye kind one to another, tenderhearted, forgiving one another, even as God for Christ's sake hath forgiven you" (Ephesians 4:31, 32).

This is the kindness that will lead us to love our enemies; bless them that curse us; do good to them that hate us and pray for them which despitefully use and persecute us, because we do not give them what they deserve, but what they need (Matthew 5:44). Then, Jesus says, ". . . . your reward shall be great, and ye shall be the children of the Highest: for he is kind unto the unthankful and to the evil" (Luke 6:35).

Love celebrates the good in others ("charity envieth not")

The term "envieth not" means "not zealous." The term comes from the word 'zeal'. The word 'zeal' or 'envy' can be used in a good sense when used to describe an "honorable emulation with the consequent imitation of that which is excellent." However, zeal, when used in the negative sense, as used here by Paul, refers to the idea of not only a desire for the good seen in others, but a desire to destroy the good that one admires (Acts 5:17; Romans 13:13; James 3:14).

Envy is the correct term to describe the evil desire that Saul cherished toward David. Saul wanted to kill David, not because David did wrong, but because he (Saul) was jealous (envious) of the good that he saw in David (see 1 Samuel 18). The Apostle Paul says, "love envieth not." In other words, love can bear the fact that others will possess different and even better qualities and talents than it possesses. Paul identified "envy" as being the main cause of quarrel and division among the Corinthian believers, in that some were thinking that their leader was better than the other, and their talent/gift was more important than the other (1 Corinthians 3:2-4; 12-14).

Love does not boast ("charity vaunteth not itself")

We derive this term from the Greek word, *perperos*, which means, "to exult in things one has." In other words, it means to be proud or "one who shows himself above his fellows." We can safely conclude, therefore, that love is not proud. Whatever talent, gifts or privileges love possesses, it should only be used to bless others and not to show oneself to be better than others. Thus, Paul knew that if love truly existed among the believers in Corinth, there would not be any argument about whose gift is better than the other. All would work together for the edifying of the Church and the preaching of the gospel.

Love is not proud ("charity. . . is not puffed up")

This term is like the previous one. Its meaning comes from the Greek word *phusioo* which means, (in the primary sense) "to inflate," and by extension, to "make proud" or "haughty." *Phusio* is the opposite of humility or meekness, which is an important attribute of love. The word of God tells us that, ". . . God resisteth the proud, but giveth grace unto the humble" (James 4:6). The proud is deceived about his/her true condition and, therefore, will not ask God for the help that he or she needs (Revelation 3:15-17). The Bible teaches that the persons whom God receives are those who have a conscious knowledge of their condition and their weaknesses and are willing, not only to ask for help, but to continually depend on God for strength and grace (Isaiah 66:1, 2; Luke 18:9-14; Psalm 51:17).

According to Ellen G. White, "Human nature is ever struggling for expression, ready for contest; but those who learn of Christ are emptied of self, of pride, of love of supremacy, and there is silence in the soul. Self is yielded to the disposal of the Holy Spirit. Then we are not anxious to have the highest place. We have no ambition to crowd and elbow ourselves into notice; but we feel that our highest place is at the feet of our Saviour."[2]

Love is not rude ("charity . . . doth not behave itself unseemly")

This expression comes from the Greek word, *askemoneou*, which comes from another Greek word which means, "to be unbecoming," "to behave self-uncomely" or "rude." In other words, love is never rude. There are many Christians who pride themselves as being abrupt and frank. However, according to Ellen G. White, such qualities are not to be considered as virtues. She writes,

"All coarseness and roughness must be put away from us. Courtesy, refinement, Christian politeness, must be cherished. Guard against being abrupt and blunt. Do not regard such peculiarities as virtues, for God does not so regard them. Endeavor not to offend any unnecessarily."[3]

In speaking about Jesus on the same topic, Ellen White also states,

"He (Jesus) was never rude, never needlessly spoke a severe word, never gave needless pain to a sensitive soul. He did not censure human weakness. He spoke the truth, but always in love. He denounced hypocrisy, unbelief, and iniquity; but tears were in His voice as He uttered His scathing rebukes."[4]

Love is not selfish ("charity . . . seeketh not her own")

This aspect of love declares that love is not selfish. It does not seek its own interest. Love forgets about its safety, convenience, and comfort in its pursuit for the good of others. "Jesus," Ellen White states, "did not count heaven a place to be desired while we were lost. He left the heavenly courts for a life of reproach and insult, and a death of shame. He who was rich in heaven's priceless treasure, became poor, that through His poverty we might be rich. We are to follow in the path He trod."[5] That is why the Apostle Paul counsels us to, "Let nothing be done through strife or vainglory; but in lowliness of mind let each esteem other better than themselves. Look not every man on his own things, but every man also on the things of others. Let this mind be in you, which was also in Christ Jesus: Who, being in the form of God, thought it not robbery to be equal with God: But made himself of no reputation, and took upon him the form of a servant, and was made in the likeness of men: And being found in fashion as a man, he humbled himself, and became obedient unto death, even the death of the cross" (Philippians 2:3-8).

Love is not boisterous (charity . . . is not easily provoked")

In the *King James Version* of the Bible, the word 'easily' in this phrase is supplied. Therefore, according to the Greek manuscript, the term should read, "love . . . is not provoked", as it is read in the *New King James Version*. In other words, love does not allow any outward or inner conflict to cause it to 'lose its cool'. Love practices complete self-control. You will not get love to respond to negative treatment in a negative way (Romans 12:21). You will not see love 'lose its cool' when things aren't going its way. You will not see love making angry outburst at its wife, children, co-worker, neighbor or anyone.

In describing the conditions and circumstances that Jesus experienced during His trial and sentencing to death, Ellen White says, "from insult to renewed insult, from mockery to mockery, twice tortured by the scourge, --all that night there had been scene after scene of a character to try the soul of man to the uttermost. Christ had not failed. He had spoken no word but that tended to glorify God"[6]. "He was oppressed, and He was afflicted, yet He opened not His mouth: He is brought as a lamb to the slaughter, and as a sheep before her shearers is dumb, so He openeth not his mouth" (Isaiah 53:7). The Apostle Peter says, "For even hereunto were ye called: because Christ also suffered for us, leaving us an example, that ye should follow his steps: Who did no sin, neither was guile found in his mouth: Who, when he was reviled, reviled not again; when he suffered, he threatened not; but committed himself to him that judgeth righteously:" (1 Peter 2:21-23).

It takes a lot of self-control to remain calm and loving under trying circumstances, but this is something that love demands. The good news is that meekness is one of the graces of the Spirit that is given to those who ask and seek for it (Galatians 5:22-23).

Love keeps no record of wrongs ("charity . . . thinketh no evil")

This expression comes from the Greek phrase, *logizetai to kakon*, "reckoning the bad thing." It is rightly rendered in the *New Living Translation*, "love . . . . keeps no record of when it has been wronged." In other words, love does not use the mistakes of others as a reason to treat them unkindly. According to Ellen White, "If we keep uppermost in our minds the unkind and unjust acts of others we shall find it impossible to love them as Christ has loved us; but if our thoughts dwell upon the wondrous love and pity of Christ for us, the same spirit will flow out to others. We should love and respect one another, notwithstanding the faults and imperfections that we cannot help seeing."[7] In commenting on this passage of Scripture, she states, "Christlike love places the most favorable construction on the motives and acts of others. It does not needlessly expose their faults; it does not listen eagerly to unfavorable reports but seeks rather to bring to mind the good qualities of others."[8]

Indeed, when we seek God's mercy, He does not use our mistakes and past sins against us. "If thou, LORD, shouldest mark iniquities," the Psalmist exclaimed, "O Lord, who shall stand? But there is forgiveness with thee, that thou mayest be feared" (Psalm 130:3, 4). The Prophet Micah also declares, "Who is a God like unto thee, that pardoneth iniquity, and passeth by the transgression of the remnant of his heritage? he retaineth not his anger for ever, because he delighteth in mercy. He will turn again, he will have compassion upon us; he will subdue our iniquities; and thou wilt cast all their sins into the depths of the sea" (Micah 7:18, 19). We should do the same for others.

Love endures all things ("charity . . . endureth all things")

The *New Living Translation* of the Bible succinctly translates this passage of Scripture as, "Love never gives up, never loses faith, is always hopeful, and endures through every circumstance." Love defines God's character. God's character was more clearly revealed to us in the life of Jesus Christ while He was on the earth. God gave the prophet Isaiah the privilege to prophesy of Jesus' character and work attitude. He said, "A bruised reed shall He not break, and the smoking flax shall He not quench: he shall bring forth judgment unto truth. He shall not fail nor be discouraged, till he have set judgment in the earth: and the isles shall wait for his law" (Isaiah 42:3, 4, NLT).

A "bruised reed" in this passage of Scripture, refers to a reed (which is used as a 'walking stick') that is so damaged that it cannot support anything or anyone without being completely broken. Also "smoking flax" refers to the wick of a lamp that has only enough fire to give off smoke; not to give light. Both these items are presented as being in a position of hopelessness. However, the Bible says, that Jesus will not break the bruised reed; neither will He quench the smoking flax. The smoking flax and the bruised reed primarily refer to the Nation of Israel, through whom God was working to "set judgment in the earth." Jesus fulfilled this prophecy in the sense that when Jesus came on earth, Israel was in such a spiritual condition that could truly be defined as "smoking flax." However, Jesus did not give up. He accepted and worked with those who received Him and through them, He set the world alight with His gospel.

Throughout Jesus' life on earth, we can see this same principle being played out, not only about Israel as a Nation; but to individuals. Often, indeed, He met people whose lives were like bruised reed and smoking flax. For example, the woman caught in adultery (John 8:1-11), the Samaritan woman (John 4), the paralytic (John 5). However, instead of breaking the bruised reed or snuff out the last breath of hope from these persons' lives, Jesus sought to restore hope and meaning to them.

Those of us who have tasted of the grace of God can truly testify that our lives have been like a bruised reed or smoking flax; but God did not give up on us. God's only intention is for us to live. As long as there is an opportunity to help us, God will. According to what He testified to the prophet Ezekiel, ". . . . As I live, saith the Lord GOD, I have no pleasure in the death of the wicked; but that the wicked turn from his way and live: turn ye, turn ye from your evil ways; for why will ye die, O house of Israel?" (Ezekiel 33:11).

Therefore, when the love of God takes control of our lives, we will have the same attitude towards those whom we meet daily. Love can look beyond people's weaknesses and mistakes and not only see what they can be in Christ, but love treats them that way. According to Ellen G. White, "Love not only bears with others' faults, but cheerfully submits to whatever suffering and inconvenience such forbearance makes necessary. This love 'never faileth.' As a precious treasure it will be carried by its possessor through the portals of the city of God."[9]

The point is, if we want to measure our progress or maturity in character, love (as defined in Scripture and reflected in the life of Christ) should be our measuring rod. Love is more than what we do—it is who we are. This is what the Holy Spirit wants to change about us—our character.

---

[1] George Knight, *My Gripe with God* (Hagerstown, Maryland: Review and Herald Publishing Association, 1990), 15.

[2] Ellen G. White, *Thus Spoke Jesus: Principles for a Harried Society* (Miami, Florida: Inter-American Division Publishing Association, 2007), 36.

[3] Ellen G. White, *Evangelism* (Hagerstown, Maryland: Review and Herald Publishing Association, 2002), 637.

[4] Ellen G. White, *Steps to Christ* (Miami, Florida: Inter-American Division Publishing Association. 2008), 7.

[5] Ellen G. White, *The Desire of Ages* (Coldwater, Michigan: Remnant Publications, 2000), 416.

[6] Ibid, 742.

[7] Ellen G. White, *Steps to Christ*, 121.

[8] Ellen G. White, *Acts of the Apostles* (Miami, Florida: Inter-American Division Publishing Association, 1911), 319.

[9] Ellen G. White, *Testimonies for the Church, vol. 5* (Miami, Florida: Inter-American Division Publishing Association, 1948), 169.

CHAPTER 4
Maturity in Faith

God works in us to form our character like Jesus';
faith keeps us in the workshop.

Whenever I talk with persons who are not Christians about their salvation, one of the main reasons they give for delaying their decisions about accepting Christ, is that they want to make sure that when they come into the Church, they do not backslide or 'turn back.' They will tell me that their greatest problem is not to start the Christian journey, but to stay the course until the end. Though the idea of delaying one's decision to accept Christ is always dangerous, I am sure we can understand the sentiment about not wanting to fail. All of us long for a consistent relationship with God. We long to break free from the cycle of sin, guilt, and repentance that many of us find ourselves in at times. Some persons even conclude that such an idea of a consistent relationship with God is too far-fetched to become a reality for them.

Have you ever wondered what the secret to a consistent relationship with God is? What is the secret to the success of men like Job, Paul, Moses, Joshua, Caleb, Elisha, Elijah, and many other…men, who were subject to like passions as we are; yet, God demonstrated His power in their lives with such consistency. We find the secret in the second dimension of the Christian life by which we measure spiritual maturity—faith.

The Apostle Paul confirmed this thought when he outlined in Hebrews 11 that it was by faith that the Elders (Patriarchs) received a good report (approval) from God.

But, what is faith and how can we have the same experience as these faithful men in the Bible? According to Hebrews 11:1, "Now faith is the substance of things hoped for, the evidence of things not seen." "Faith is trusting God—believing that He loves us and knows best what is for our good. . . . Our lives, ourselves, are already His (God's); faith acknowledges His ownership and accepts its blessing"[1]. In other words, faith broadens our outlook on life to take in the realm of the unseen realities presented to us in the Word of God (Romans 10:17). Faith, simply put, is how we accept and hold to the things of God. The things of God come to us by revelation -- through the Scriptures and Nature (Romans 10:17; Romans 1:19-21; Psalm 19:1-7). It is necessary to exercise faith because many of the things revealed in the Word of God are invisible (2 Corinthians 4:18).

Paul mentioned that it is by faith we have come to believe and accept that God created the world — His Word (Hebrews 11:3). Most of all, we have been saved by exercising faith in the merits and atoning sacrifice of Jesus Christ for salvation and by faith we keep our hold on God (Ephesians 2:8, 9; Hebrews 10:35-39).

The truth is, as we walk the Christian pathway, we are often tempted to give up on our faith in God and to loosen our hold on Him. Once we are doing this—doubting God to the point of questioning His love for us, it suggests that something is "lacking in [your] faith"; it means that we are not yet made perfect in faith (*see* 1 Thessalonians 3:10; James 1:2-4 *margin*). A mature faith is one that is constant and unwavering in its hold on the things of God. According to the Apostle James, ". . . . he that wavereth [in his faith] is like a wave of the sea driven with the wind and tossed.

For let not that man think that he shall receive anything of the Lord. A double minded man is unstable in all his ways" (James 1:6-8 margin). We are not saying that a person with mature faith will always get what he or she requests of God. The Apostle James is here referring to one's confidence in God's love and power.

While Jesus was on earth with His disciples, "lack of faith" was one of the main problems He had with them. Jesus longed to have His disciples trust in Him, not only sometimes, but all the time. Often you would hear Him upbraid His disciples, "O ye of little faith," "why did you doubt?", "faithless generation," "have faith in God," and so on. Jesus knew that for them to be truly blessed and to accomplish the work He had for them to do, the disciples needed to be mature in faith; they needed to exercise a constant and abiding trust in God, even in the face of difficulty (see Luke 18:1-8). Paul also pointed out that most of the Israelites who traversed the wilderness for forty (40) years, did not enter God's rest because of unbelief. "For unto us was the gospel preached, as well as unto them: but the word preached did not profit them, not being mixed with faith in them that heard it" (Hebrews 4:2). The problem with the Israelites in the wilderness experience was not that they did not believe that God was with them, but that their belief did not benefit them.

When they saw God's miracles, they would rejoice in the knowledge of His presence, power, love and wisdom, but when they faced difficulty they chose not to depend on or trust in God's love—they gave in to doubt and discouragement (see Psalm 106). "Wherefore" says the Lord, "I was grieved with that generation, and said, they do alway err in their heart; and they have not known my ways. So I sware in my wrath, They shall not enter into my rest.) Take heed, brethren, lest there be in any of you an evil heart of unbelief, in departing from the living God." (Heb 3:10-12). Paul told the believers that the only way to truly partake of Christ is if "we hold the beginning of our confidence steadfast unto the end;" (Hebrews 3:14).

Here is what it means to be mature in faith—to have constant and unswerving confidence in God (see Hebrews 10:34-38). In the heart that is made perfect in faith, there is an abiding trust, a rest in God, that is produced by what we know about Him in His word and according to what we have experienced in our walk with Him. Here is the faith that will lead to obedience in all things. According to Ellen G. White, no great experience can substitute for the need to be mature or consistent in our faith in God:

"It is not a conclusive evidence that a man is a Christian because he manifests spiritual ecstasy under extraordinary circumstances. Holiness is not rapture: it is an entire surrender of the will to God; it is living by every word that proceeds from the mouth of God; it is doing the will of our heavenly Father; it is trusting God in trial, in darkness as well as in the light; it is walking by faith and not by sight; it is relying on God with unquestioning confidence, and resting in His love."[2]

To experience maturity in faith there are certain things about God that our faith should accept/take hold of and never doubt. These are like pillars on which we build a strong faith. These pillars are:

1. Accepting that God is.

2. Accepting who God is.

3. Accepting our obligations to God and our fellowmen.

Faith accepts that God is

Faith begins here. Faith begins with accepting that God exists. According to the Bible, "...he that cometh to God must believe that *He is*..." (Hebrews 11:6 emphasis supplied). The basis for our faith in God is the evidences that He has provided for us in His word and nature (Romans 10:17; Psalm 19:1-3; Romans 1:19-20). It is not our faith in God that causes Him to exist; faith only accepts the fact of His existence based on the evidence given. To have solid spiritual growth, this is something that faith must accept and hold to unwaveringly.

Accepting that God exists might seem like a truth that needs no reinforcement, but it's amazing to note that most of the times when tragedy strikes, this is one of the first questions that we ask, "where is/was God?" One Sabbath morning I was in church attending a Sabbath School Lesson study class. I was sharing an experience of God's goodness and why I believe in Him. I shared the experience of how one day I needed to go to work but did not have any money, and so I prayed to the Lord and asked Him to provide transportation for me. After I prayed, I went out to where I usually take the taxi. As soon as I went out, I was able to get a drive to work - free of cost. After sharing this experience, some of the members of the class were praising God with me, but there was one gentleman who appeared quite skeptical. He asked me, "what about the Muslim and people of other religions who pray to their gods and get similar responses, how do you explain to them that they are not serving the true God?" It was a tough question, but, now I am looking at it, it was a good one because it forced me to think about the basis for my faith in God. Do I believe in God because of the good things that He has done, or do I believe in Him simply because He is? Then the Holy Spirit gave me this answer. I said, "even if God did not provide transportation for me that morning, He would still be God."

There have been so many who have given up on their faith, simply because God did not meet their expectations. Therefore, I want to reiterate, that before faith accepts who God is (about His goodness; His power; His love), faith should accept that God is. Accepting God's existence is one of the pillars that hold up the faith of mature Christians especially in times of difficulty.

Faith accepts who God is

On the other hand, for us to experience and maintain spiritual growth, faith needs to go further than believing that God exists.

According to the Apostle James, "Thou believest that there is one God; thou doest well: the devils also believe, and tremble" (James 2:19). To have a faith that is more advanced than the devils', you also need to accept, not only that God exists, but what He is capable of and the claims that He makes on your life. Therefore, faith goes further to accept who God is, about His character and ability. It would be impossible to outline all of God's attributes in one place, however for this book, I will give some examples of some of God's attributes that faith needs to be aware of and hold on to, to experience growth and maturity. Faith needs to accept that God is omnipresent, omniscient, omnipotent, faithful to His promises and that He loves us unconditionally.

God is everywhere you need Him

"Lord, if You had been here, my brother would not have died" (John 11:21, 32 NKJV). These are the words that both Mary and Martha met Jesus with when He appeared on the scene after their brother's death four days later. Mary and Martha thought that the reason their brother had died was not that Jesus could not have healed him (they knew He was all-powerful); or that He did not care (they knew He loved them); but that He was not there (He was absent).

How often, like Mary and Martha, we forget that God is not limited by space and time. Therefore, in the face of difficulty, though we know that God loves us, that He is all-powerful, we fail to accept that He is there with us, even in times of trouble. Faith needs the assurance of God's omnipresence—He is everywhere. He can and will be anywhere we need Him at any time. We must accept and believe that if something doesn't happen the way we anticipate, it is not because God was not there.

Regarding God's omnipresence, the Psalmist David declares, "Where can I go from Your Spirit? Or where can I flee from Your presence? If I ascend into heaven, You are there; If I make my bed in hell, behold, You are there. If I take the wings of the morning, and dwell in the uttermost parts of the sea, Even there Your hand shall lead me, and Your right hand shall hold me" (Psalm 139:7-10).

The word of God tells us that when Joseph was taken to Egypt as a slave, away from his father's house, that "the Lord was with Joseph" (Genesis 39:2). And it was this consciousness of God's presence that kept Joseph's commitment to Him. God's omnipresence is not only to console us in times of trouble but to inspire consistent obedience.

It was because the children of Israel lost their sense of God's presence that they were led into idolatry at the foot of the mountain while Moses was talking with God (Exodus 32). The children of Israel had recently trembled at the visible manifestation of God's presence, when He appeared to them in a cloud on top of Mount Sinai, declaring to them the Ten Commandments (see Exodus 20:1-18). They were so terrified at the awesomeness of God's presence that they told Moses, "Speak thou with us, and we will hear: but let not God speak with us, lest we die" (Exodus 20:19). And Moses responded by saying, "Fear not: for God is come to prove you, and that his fear may be before your faces, that ye sin not" (v. 20). In other words, God revealed Himself to the people, not to frighten them, but to make them aware of His power, presence, and holiness, so that they would always recognize their obligation to Him. However, as soon as Moses went up into the mountain with God, the people got tired of waiting for him to come back. "And when the people saw that Moses delayed coming down out of the mount, the people gathered themselves together unto Aaron, and said unto him, Up, make us gods, which shall go before us; for as for this Moses, the man that brought us up out of the land of Egypt, we wot not what is become of him" (Exodus 32:1). In other words, the people saw God as being "in the mountain." They did not recognize that though they were not hearing His literal voice from Heaven or seeing the lightning and thunder, that God was with them and that they were as much obligated to obey Him as when they saw the visible manifestation of His presence.

God knows everything

God's Omniscience is connected to His Omnipresence, for if He is everywhere, it is easy to see why He would know everything (which is the meaning of Omniscience). Faith needs to know that God knows everything. He knows the past, present, and future. He knows our thoughts. He knows everything that we have ever done in our lives. He knows, Jesus says, even the very number of hairs on our head (see Luke 12:7). "O Lord, You have searched me and known me" the Psalmist exclaims. "You know my sitting down and my rising; You understand my thought afar off. You comprehend my path and my lying down, and are acquainted with all my ways. There is not a word on my tongue, but behold, O Lord, You know it all together" (Psalm 139:1-4).

If we understand and appreciate how much God knows, we would not be as faithless and worried as we are sometimes. I had an experience that helped to cement my faith in God's omniscience. While attending University, I also worked at a Company in Manchester, Jamaica. I remember one semester I had a class that would begin at 1:30 pm two days for the week, but on Fridays, it would begin at 12:30 pm. Usually, on the day of that class, I would travel to school with a co-worker, who happened to be doing the same class that I was doing.

On this Friday, there was a major examination for the course. This examination was so important that the teacher said if we should fail it, it's very unlikely that we would pass the course. Added to that, if I failed this course (because it is a preparation for another course), I would be held back by at least a whole year in University. I, therefore, took much time to prepare and study for the exam. Usually, because the class was at 1:30 pm, I was able to have lunch between 12:00 noon and 12:30 pm and take time to prepare to travel to school. That is exactly what I was doing this

Friday, forgetting that instead of 1:30 pm, because it was a Friday, the class would begin at 12:30 pm. At about 1:00 pm, after I was done with lunch and now prepared to leave, I called my co-worker on the telephone to ask if he was ready for school. I rang his office phone and did not get an answer. I was a little concerned, but not at the point of worrying because I said to myself, maybe he is just not at the desk or on another call. Therefore, knowing that the time for the class was due and wanting to eliminate any doubt, I went to his office to find out what was happening. When I went to his office, his chair was empty, and his desk was cleared as if he had already left.

Now, my knees started shaking, and beads of sweat began popping up all over my palms because now I couldn't even imagine that what I am thinking might be true. It was then I realized what was happening—it was Friday, and I was half (½) hour late for the exam. But then I said to myself, "I serve a good God; He wouldn't let this happen to me. Maybe God allowed it to happen that the exam hasn't started yet, and I can probably take a taxi and get there to do it on time." Therefore, I went and called the school (specifically the computer lab) to find out if the exam had started. It was then that I heard what I did not want to hear—the exam had started half (½) hour ago!! And it would be impossible for me to make it because I was not only ½ hour late, but half (½) hour away from school.

I began to feel depressed, discouraged, disappointed and all the negative emotions that you can describe. I felt a heavy load coming over me; heavier than I could handle.

But then the thought came to me, "is it right for me to feel this way?" I have always been telling people that according to the Apostle Paul, they should be "anxious for nothing, but in everything by prayer and supplication, with thanksgiving, let your requests be made known to God; and the peace of God, which surpasses all understanding, will guard your hearts and minds through Christ Jesus" (Philippians 4:6, 7). "Now," I thought, "is it that there are certain situations in which it is okay to be worried?" or "is it that there is something I need to learn?"

In response to my concerns, the Holy Spirit brought these questions into my mind, "while I was there studying, was God watching me? While I was there at 12:30 pm, still sitting down, enjoying my lunch, while the exam that was so important to me, had already begun, was God seeing all of that? The answer came back to me, "yes, God was watching, and He knew I was late." So, if the answer was yes, then the other question was, "was God worried to death?" "Was God worried about what's going to happen if I didn't do the exam?" Then, I thought, "if God saw everything that happened, knowing that I sincerely forgot about the time change for the exam, and He wasn't worried, why should I be worried?"

It was at that point that I decided that I was not going to worry; I was going to follow what Paul says in Philippians 4:6, 7, present my case to God and leave it there. I did just that, and I stopped worrying to the point where I was able to enjoy my weekend without any thought about school and what I was going to do about missing the exam.

Now, the story doesn't end there. On Monday when I went to the class, the teacher had already marked the papers and was returning them to the students. The teacher then announced that the grades for the exam were so bad, that he had decided to give a second exam (later) and he would use the better of both grades as our course grade. I know you might think I was jumping and praising God at that time, but no, not really. I had already been praising God and giving Him thanks. I had already gotten the victory over worry and fretting. Why? Because, according to Hagar, Abraham's maid, we serve a God who sees—a God who is always watching over us and seeking to do us good (Genesis 16:13). Now, my confidence was not in the good news that the teacher brought—that I got a second chance at doing the test— my confidence was in a God, who is not only all-powerful, all-loving and is everywhere, but a God who sees and knows everything that I am going through.

Like Job, our confidence in God's omniscience will lead us to accept that because God knows, and He can do, we can be confident that if we are faithful to Him, He will work everything out for our good (Job 23:9, 10; Romans 8:28).

God can do all that He promises

If we should accept that God is always with us (omnipresent) and that He knows everything (omniscient) about us, without accepting that He can do anything (omnipotent) for us, our faith would still be lacking something. Whenever we fail to accept and hold unwaveringly to God's omnipotence, we will fall into the same trap that Abraham did in trying to "help out" God (Genesis 16).

The Bible gives us so many instructions on God's omnipotence. "And Jesus came and spake unto them, saying, all power is given unto me in heaven and in earth" (Matthew 28:18). "For with God nothing shall be impossible" (Luke 1:37; Matthew 19:26). There are very few people who doubt these things, in theory, the problem is with believing and holding to them in times of difficulty.

For example, when the children of Israel faced the Red Sea with Pharaoh's armies behind them; when they experienced thirst and hunger in the wilderness and when the journey seemed impossible to continue, they doubted and complained against God because they forgot and failed to put confidence in God's Omnipotence.

The question is, can we still believe that God is omnipotent when we are threatened when we are about to lose our job, when faced with marital and financial troubles? Faith leads us to not only accept these things but to trust God.

God is faithful

We can be aware of God's omnipresence, omniscience, omnipotence, yet we do not benefit from a relationship with Him unless we have the assurance that He is faithful to His promises. Therefore, trusting God's faithfulness is a very important element of our faith in Him. It is God's faithfulness that leads Him to fulfill His promises always, once we meet the conditions. All of God's plans to help us are in His word through His promises.

To assure Noah that He will not again destroy the earth with a flood, God placed a bow in the cloud (Genesis 9:13-15). God said to Noah, "I do set my bow in the cloud, and it shall be for a token of a covenant between me and the earth. And it shall come to pass, when I bring a cloud over the earth, that the bow shall be seen in the cloud: And I will remember my covenant, which |is| between me and you and every living creature of all flesh; and the waters shall no more become a flood to destroy all flesh."

Even after over 4,000 years, God has kept His promise to the earth, that He will not destroy it with a flood anymore. God has always been anxious for us to understand and put confidence in His faithfulness. When He wanted to assure Abraham of His faithfulness, God made an oath (Hebrews 6:16-20). The oath is significant, in that during the time of Abraham and the Patriarchs, the act of swearing or taking an oath was a means of establishing that something was true (Numbers 5:18-20). For example, if a man gave something to his friend to keep, like an animal or any personal property, and when he returns, the animal died, in order to resolve the case both would appear before the Elders and the man who kept his friends goods, would be made to swear that he did not touch it, and they would accept the oath as truth. This process could work because swearing would mean that God is your witness; and if God is your witness, then what you say must be true (Exodus 22:10, 11). That is why God appealed to Israel not to take His name in vain or to swear by His name falsely (Exodus 20:16).

Now, God did not have anyone greater than Himself by which

to swear; therefore, He swore by Himself to Abraham that blessing He will bless Him. This promise is the promise of salvation through Jesus Christ. God places His reputation at stake to assure us of the immutability of His promises. Jesus said it is easier for heaven and earth to pass away, than for one of God's promises to fail (Matthew 24:35). This is the assurance that we have that God is faithful.

Because of God's faithfulness to His word, when we claim His promises, once we meet the conditions, we do not need to wait to feel that we receive what we ask, we can go away with the assurance that God will or has fulfilled His word. That is why, memorizing scripture (especially His promises) is an important skill that helps to strengthen our faith in God's faithfulness.

God loves us unconditionally

Faith must also accept God's unconditional love for us, to know that God would do nothing to harm us. Faith must believe that God's motive towards us is always one of love and kindness. God never intends to do us harm. "For I know the thoughts that I think toward you, saith the LORD, thoughts of peace, and not of evil, to give you an expected end" (Jeremiah 29:11). ". . . .[As] I live, saith the Lord GOD, I have no pleasure in the death of the wicked; but that the wicked turn from his way and live: turn ye, turn ye from your evil ways; for why will ye die, O house of Israel?" (Ezekiel 33:11).

Knowing and believing that God loves us always will help us to endure temptations and trials, especially when the Devil launches attacks on us and tries to blame God for it. A perfect example of this is that of the experience of Job. Satan destroyed Job's property, afflicted him with leprosy and attempted (through Job's wife) to blame God for all these things, but Job's faith in God's love did not fail. "In all this," the Bible says, "Job sinned not, nor charged God foolishly" (Job 1:22). Job knew that God has no evil intentions towards him; and even if He allowed these things to happen, it would eventually work to His glory and for Job's best interest (Job

23:9, 10; Romans 8:28).

Faith Accepts our obligation to obey God

Now, Job's experience is a very powerful illustration of this final element of faith--it is Job's faith in God's power, presence, knowledge, faithfulness, love, and wisdom that led Job to remain faithful to God, even in times of difficulties. "My foot hath held his steps" Job testified, "His way have I kept, and not declined. Neither have I gone back from the commandment of his lips; I have esteemed the words of his mouth more than my necessary |*food*|" (Job 23:11, 12).

This is the part of faith that most persons have a problem with -- the part of obedience to God. That is why Jesus asked, "And why call ye me, Lord, Lord, and do not the things which I say?" (Luke 6:46). Constantly, Jesus emphasized the point that those who are God's children, simply put, are those who "hear the word of God, and do it" (Luke 8:21; 11:28).

The greatest demonstration of our faith in God and who He is, is that we obey His word. Because God is everywhere, I should respect Him. Because He knows everything, even my thoughts, I must honor Him always. Because He can do all things – I am never out of strength to do His will (I have no excuse). Then I must obey Him under all circumstances. My obedience is what demonstrates that I truly believe these things about God.

It was Abraham's faith in God's presence, power, love, wisdom, and faithfulness that led him to obey the Lord in going to sacrificing his son as a burnt sacrifice, simply because God said it (Hebrews 11:17-19).

---

[1] Ellen G. White, *Education* (Ontario, Canada: Pacific Press Publishing Association, 1903, 1952), 253.

[2] Ellen G. White, *Acts of the Apostles*, 51.

CHAPTER 5
Maturity in Understanding

God works in us to transform our characters into His likeness (love);
Faith keeps us in the workshop;
Understanding gives us reasons to stay in the workshop

Love is the fruit of our connection with God; faith keeps us connected, and understanding gives us reason to remain connected.

Understanding is a dimension of the Christian life that is not as expounded on as faith and love, but it also plays an important role in determining our maturity. Understanding refers to our ability to "see" the things of God. The opposite of understanding is referred to in the Bible as "darkness," "blindness" or "hardness of heart." 1 Corinthians 2:14; 2 Corinthians 4:4-6. This aspect of the Christian life corresponds with what Jesus spoke about when He says, "he that hath an ear to hear, let him hear" (Matthew 13:13-16).

It is our understanding of the things of God that leads us to put our faith in Him. Therefore, the more we understand God and the things of God, the more we grow to trust Him.

For example, a child will complain and murmur about going to school, going to bed early, washing the dishes and performing other duties in the home. But when this child becomes an adult, he or she will choose to do these same things without coercion or force. Why? Not because these things have become more fun to do, but because the child now understands the value of responsibility and the need for a good education; he or she now sees things from the perspective of his/her parents.

So, it is in the Christian's life, a lack of understanding of the things of God will lead us to complain about trials, temptations and the hardness of the Christian's life. But when through the study of God's word, revelation by the Holy Spirit and practical experience in obeying the word of God, we become mature in our understanding, we will have a changed attitude towards doing the will of God.

The Apostle Paul highlighted that it is immaturity in understanding that leads to inconsistency in faith (Ephesians 4:13-15; Hebrews 5:12–6:3).

Now, while as Christians, we will continually advance in our understanding of God, to be mature and consistent in our faith, some basic teachings are fundamental to our faith. Paul hinted some of them in his counsel to the Hebrews, "For when for the time ye ought to be teachers, ye have need that one teach you again which [be] the *first principles* of the oracles of God; and are become such as have need of milk, and not of strong meat" (Hebrews 5:12, emphasis supplied).

The Apostle Paul here refers to some doctrines as being the "first principles" of the oracles of God. In the next chapter, he highlighted some of these doctrines that are among the "first principles." He said, "Therefore leaving the principles of the doctrine of Christ, let us go on unto perfection; not laying again the foundation of repentance from dead works, and of faith toward God, of the doctrine of baptisms, and of laying on of hands, and of resurrection of the dead, and of eternal judgment. And this will we do if God permit." (Hebrews 6:1-3).

The Apostle Paul was saying to the Jewish believers, "these are doctrines that you should have known and are certain of already."

51

The fact that they needed to be taught these things repeatedly meant that they were making little progress in their Christian experience and were not mature.

Here, I would like to outline some of the doctrines that would form part of the "first principles" that establishes a strong Christian experience. I am not proposing to explain these doctrines intricately; I will give a brief overview and then will focus on how an understanding of these doctrines help with the stability of our faith. For an extensive exposition of these doctrines, you can read the *Seventh-day Adventist Believe: An exposition of the fundamental beliefs of the Seventh-day Adventist Church, 2nd Ed. 2005* published by the General Conference of the Seventh-day Adventists Church.

The Nature of Man

An experience I had with one of my first employers, whom I will call Mr. T, led me to think and study more about this doctrine—the doctrine of man. Mr. T, who was not a Christian, was a very kind person. He helped several young men (including myself) to find jobs, skill and to have a start in life. While working with him, the doctors diagnosed Mr. T with a terminal disease.

Since I was a Christian, Mr. T would at times ask me questions about my faith and religion. I tried my best to answer, and though I probably did not always have an answer, Mr. T, for some reason, always felt confident to ask. During the time of his illness, Mr. T asked me a question that rested on my mind for some time. He asked me (I will paraphrase) "why do you think God allows these things to happen to me?" "The fact that I have been such a good person to so many, don't you think God should consider sparing me these inconveniences?" Mr. T felt that being a "good person" was enough to grant him favor with God. In a sense, he felt it was a little unfair for God to ignore his "good works" and for him to be treated this way. I don't quite remember the answer that I gave, except that I know the story of Job (in the Bible) came up in the conversation.

Trying to find Biblical answers for Mr. T's question has helped me to appreciate the importance of understanding the doctrine of man or the nature of man, especially considering his need for salvation. A clear understanding of the doctrine of man will help to put some things into perspective regarding man's relationship to God; man's limitations; what to expect of him and how sin has affected man's ability to please God.

According to the Bible, God created man in His image. The Genesis account of man's creation reads thus, "And God said, Let us make man in our image, after our likeness: and let them have dominion over the fish of the sea, and over the fowl of the air, and over the cattle, and over all the earth, and over every creeping thing that creepeth upon the earth. So, God created man in his [own] image, in the image of God created he him; male and female created he them" (Genesis 1:26, 27). According to E. G. White, "Man was originally endowed with noble powers and a well-balanced mind. He was perfect in his being, and in harmony with God. His thoughts were pure, his aims holy"[1]. "His nature was in harmony with the will of God. His mind can comprehend divine things. His affections were pure; his appetites and passions were under the control of reason. He was holy and happy in bearing the image of God and in perfect obedience to his will."[2]

Ellen G. White also said, "through disobedience, his (man's) powers were perverted, and selfishness took the place of love. His nature became so weakened through transgression that it was impossible for him, in his strength, to resist the power of evil. He was made captive by Satan and would have remained so forever had not God specially interposed."[3]

This fallen nature is referred to in the Bible as "the flesh" or "the carnal mind". According to the Apostle Paul, "For to be carnally minded [is] death; but to be spiritually minded [is] life and peace. Because the carnal mind [is] enmity against God: for it is not subject to the law of God, neither indeed can be. So then they that are in the flesh cannot please God" (Romans 8:6-8).

That is why Jesus told Nicodemus, "Verily, verily, I say unto thee, Except a man be born again, he cannot see the kingdom of God" (John 3:3). For man that is born of a woman to please God, he must have a transforming experience by the Holy Spirit, referred to in the Bible as being "born again" (Job 25:4).

Without being "born again," no amount of "good works" can restore us to good standing with God. According to Ellen G. White, "It is impossible for us, of ourselves, to escape from the pit of sin in which we are sunken . . . . Education, culture, the exercise of the will, human effort . . . . may produce outward correctness of behavior, but they cannot change the heart; they cannot purify the springs of life. There must be a power working from within, a new life from above, before men can be changed from sin to holiness."[4]

When we accept Christ through repentance and confession of sins, God gives us His Holy Spirit, so that we are not only considered "justified," but we receive power to walk in obedience to His word in a way that is pleasing to Him. According to the Apostle Paul, "[There is] therefore now no condemnation to them which are in Christ Jesus, who walk not after the flesh, but after the Spirit. For the law of the Spirit of life in Christ Jesus hath made me free from the law of sin and death. For what the law could not do, in that it was weak through the flesh, God sending his own Son in the likeness of sinful flesh, and for sin, condemned sin in the flesh: That the righteousness of the law might be fulfilled in us, who walk not after the flesh, but after the Spirit" (Romans 8:1-4).

If the Christian continues to put his faith in Jesus, depend on the Holy Spirit and walk in obedience to God's word, he will remain faithful. Once we continue to "abide in Christ", all will be well, but we must always keep in mind what Jesus said, "without Me, you can do nothing." In other words, when a person comes to Christ, he or she is always free to turn from dependence on Christ and return to walk in the flesh. That is why the Apostle Paul reminded the Roman believers, "Therefore, brethren, we are debtors, not to the flesh, to live after the flesh. For if ye live after the flesh, ye shall die: but if ye through the Spirit do mortify the deeds of the body, ye shall live" (Romans 8:12, 13). Also, he upbraided the believers in Galatia, "O foolish Galatians, who hath bewitched you, that ye should not obey the truth, before whose eyes Jesus Christ hath been set forth, crucified among you? This only would I learn of you, Received ye the Spirit by the works of the law, or by the hearing of faith? Are ye so foolish? having begun in the Spirit, are ye now made perfect by the flesh?" (Galatians 3:1-3).

The truth is, when we come to Christ, walking by His Spirit and experiencing success in the Christian life, we are often tempted to interpret this success as a sign that we are now able to live the Christian life on our own. However, if we understood the doctrine of man's nature and his need for salvation, we will be sure to abide in Christ, not only sometimes, but all the time. According to Ellen G. White, "We cannot keep ourselves from sin for one moment. Every moment we are dependent upon God"[5]. Therefore, "those who have felt the sanctifying power of the Holy Spirit and have tasted of the good life to come, should not think that they are sinless; that they have reached the highest state of perfection, and are beyond the reach of temptation."[6]

It is an understanding of the doctrine of man's need for salvation that helps us to remain humble and dependent on God.

The Great Controversy

I once read an interesting statement about prayer in the book, The Kneeling Christian, that goes like this, "If there was no devil there would be no difficulty in prayer."[7] This statement expresses the sentiments of questions that many Christians have echoed over the years, "if God is so loving, why is it so hard to serve Him? Why do so much unfairness and evil exist in a world? If we have such good intentions of wanting to obey God, why do we get so much opposition? Why can't people get along with each other?"

A clear understanding of the doctrine of the Great Controversy will help to answer these questions and settle our faith in God. The Bible teaches that though God created this world/universe, there are forces in operation, seen and unseen, that are working contrary and in opposition to the government of God (see Ephesians 6:10-12).

The Bible teaches that God made this universe and its creatures perfect and loving. But rebellion found its way in the heart of one who was among the most exalted and powerful of God's angels—Lucifer (Ezekiel 28:11-19; Isaiah 14:12-14). Lucifer turned Satan and the Devil, by lying, accusations, and deceptions, led one-third (1/3) of the angels in heaven in rebellion against God. This led to "war in heaven" -- the war between Satan and his angels and the Son of God and his angels (Revelation 12:7-11). Satan and his angels were given the opportunity to repent and turn to God, but when God realized that they would not, they were cast out of heaven (2 Peter 2:4).

When God created this world, the Controversy had started already. God was about to create a free-thinking, moral being—man. This earth would, therefore, become an arena to see the outworking of both principles—good and evil. God created man perfect, gave him all he needed for life and sustenance. Man was given a test to see whether he would obey the Word of God or follow the deceptions of Satan (Genesis 2:16, 17). God told man specifically that he should not eat of the tree of the knowledge of good and evil. Satan appeared to Eve in the form of a serpent, and by lies and deception, cunningly led Eve (and eventually Adam) into disobedience (Genesis 3:1-6).

Because of disobeying God's Word, several things happened to man and to this world:

1. Man became lawful captives of Satan (John 8:44);

2. Man became a slave to sin—his nature became fallen (John 8:34);

3. The intimate relationship between God and man was now ruptured—man's heart was now at enmity with God (Isaiah 59:1, 2; Genesis 3:23, 24).

4. Man became mortal—subject to death (Genesis 3:19; Romans 5:12);

5. This world was subject to corruption (Romans 8:19-22; Genesis 3:17, 18).

It took the incarnation, life, death, resurrection and mediatory work of Jesus (the Son of God) to not only deliver man from the power of sin, Satan and death, but to vindicate God's character, destroy the works of the Devil, and to reconcile man to God (1 John 3:8; Hebrews 2:14, 15; John 3:16; 2 Corinthians 5:18-20).

Though Satan's fate has been sealed, the Great Controversy will continue until the close of the Judgment (during which time God's people and His character will be vindicated, and the wicked and Satan will be condemned to eternal destruction) (see Revelation 20:11-14).

It is within the context of this Controversy that we are asked to carry on our relationship with God. It is, therefore, important to have a clear understanding of the issues in the Controversy. A clear understanding of the doctrine of the Great Controversy will:

1. *Produces in us a constant state of watchfulness.* "An understanding of this doctrine convicts one of the needs to combat evil. Success is possible only through dependence on Jesus Christ, the Captain of the hosts, the One 'strong and mighty, the Lord mighty in battle' (Ps. 24:8)."[8].

2. *Explains/ the mystery of suffering.* "Evil did not originate with God. He who 'loved righteousness and hated lawlessness' (Heb. 1:9) is not to blame for the world's misery. Satan, the fallen angel, is responsible for cruelty and suffering. We can better understand robberies, murders, funerals, crimes, accidents—however heartbreaking—when we see them in the framework of the great controversy"[9].

3. *Gives us confidence in our battle against evil.* As we recognize that Christ has conquered Satan and made provision for all who are willing to overcome the Devil, then though we are vigilant, we do not live our lives in fear of the Devil and what he can do to us (1 Corinthians 10:13; Hebrews 2:14, 15; Romans 8:37).

The Life, Death, and Resurrection of Christ

The incarnation, perfect life, atoning sacrifice, resurrection and mediatory work of Jesus Christ form the essence of God's response to sin and indicate to man that salvation is provided. Since the fall of man and the entrance of sin into the world, this has been the main message that God has for the world (Genesis 3:15).

God has one message for humanity, "For God so loved the world, that he gave his only begotten Son, that whosoever believeth in him should not perish, but have everlasting life" (John 3:16). It is important for us to know that in Christ's atoning work, we have:

1. *A complete justification for our sins* (Romans 8:1). For Christ took our guilt upon Himself and died as if He had committed our sins, so that we can go free of condemnation (Isaiah 53:5-7; 2 Corinthians 5:21). When we exercise faith in His name, we are covered with His righteous character (Romans 3:24).

2. *A perfect example of what it means to obey the commandments of God—the righteousness of God is revealed.* Jesus demonstrated that though it is impossible for man (on his own) to obey the law of God, it is possible for human beings, through faith in His name, to live a perfect life of obedience to the law of God.

3. *God's means of reconciling the world/universe unto Himself* (2 Corinthians 5:18-20; Colossians 1:20).

4. *Man's only means of salvation from sin.* According to Acts 4:12, "Neither is there salvation in any other: for there is none other name under heaven given among men, whereby we must be saved."

Understanding that Jesus is our Saviour and what His atonement does for us will:

1. Prevent us from adopting a legalistic religion—one that is based solely on works of human inventions.

2. Help us to trust more freely in the grace of God, rather than in any other means of salvation.

3. Help us to know that we are never too sinful to find salvation and forgiveness with God.

The Experience of Salvation

To experience freedom from guilt is a desire that has driven the spiritual journey of humanity for centuries. Men have invented all manner of methods and ideas about how to "appease the gods" and experience peace. Even within the Christian Church, for over a century, most of Christendom had lost sight of the Biblical principle of salvation. Countless spurious inventions took the place of the pure Biblical doctrine on salvation, including the "Indulgences" (where persons were taught that they could pay for full remission of sins with money, or by enlisting in the pontiff's army)[10]. In describing the conditions that existed in the church during the times of the Waldenses and the Dark Ages, Ellen G. White writes: -

".... under the guidance of pope and priest, multitudes were vainly endeavoring to obtain pardon by afflicting their bodies for the sin of their souls. Taught to trust to their good works to save them, they were ever looking to themselves, their minds dwelling upon their sinful condition, seeing themselves exposed to the wrath of God, afflicting soul and body, yet finding no relief. Thus conscientious souls were bound by the doctrines of Rome. Thousands abandoned friends and kindred, and spent their lives in convent cells. By oft-repeated fasts and cruel scourgings, by midnight vigils, by prostration for weary hours upon the cold, damp stones of their dreary abode, by long pilgrimages, by humiliating penance and fearful torture, thousands vainly sought to obtain peace of conscience. Oppressed with a sense of sin, and haunted with the fear of God's avenging wrath, many suffered on, until exhausted nature gave way, and without one ray of light or hope they sank into the tomb."[11]

Even today, centuries after the "Dark Ages," persons are often confused about how to overcome guilt; how to find peace with God.

A clear understanding of the Biblical doctrine of salvation helps us to deal with the problem of guilt correctly and maturely.

Based on the doctrine of man, we understand that because of man's fallen nature, there is nothing that he can do of himself to overcome Satan and sin. In such condition, man cannot even diagnose his spiritual status without the help of the Holy Spirit. The process of salvation begins when the Holy Spirit impresses the heart and mind with an awareness of sin and our need for salvation (John 16:8; Acts 2:37). As we look upon our condition and realize our hopelessness, the Holy Spirit reveals to our mind the love of God in giving His Son Jesus Christ to die in our behalf, so that we can exercise faith in His merits to find pardon. As we look upon the spotless Lamb of God, we see that, ". . . He [was] wounded for our transgressions, [he was] bruised for our iniquities:" (Isaiah 53:5), and we long to be set free from sin, we long to be separated from the sins that separate us from God, therefore, we not only confess our sins, but we repent of all the wrongs that we have done and ask God to forgive us and have mercy upon us (see Psalm 51). According to the Bible, "If we confess our sins, he [God] is faithful and just to forgive us [our] sins, and to cleanse us from all unrighteousness" (1 John 1:9 margin). God takes away the filthiness of our sins and covers us with the righteousness of Christ's character (Isaiah 6:6, 7; Zechariah 3:4).

Because of this transaction, man is accepted in the beloved, and is "born again." "Which . . . . [are] born, not of blood, nor of the will of the flesh, nor of the will of man, but of God" (John 1:12, 13 margins). The Bible says, ". . . If any man [be] in Christ, [he is] a new creature: old things are passed away; behold, all things are become new" (2 Cor 5:17). Man is now free from guilt, he is now free from the condemnation of his past life of sin and he stands before God justified (just as if he had never sinned) (Romans 8:1).

Not only that, but man also receives the Holy Spirit as a down payment for eternal life, and power to do the will of God and live a life that is pleasing to Him (Ephesians 1:13, 14). In other words, man receives a "new heart" --a heart that is in harmony with the will of God (Ezekiel 36:26, 27). The entire experience of salvation is a gift from God and man receive this gift by faith (Ephesians 2:8-10).

A clear understanding of the doctrine of salvation is to:

1. Prevent us from being overcome with guilt and the fear of being lost. While we walk the Christian pathway, we can fall into the temptation of thinking that we have done too much wrong for the Lord to forgive us. However, the doctrine of salvation should fuel our faith with understanding and give us victory over these negative feelings (Revelation 12:10).

2. Assure us of eternal life and being at peace with God.

Christ's Ministry in the Heavenly Sanctuary

Since He ascended to Heaven, Jesus started working as our High Priest in the heavenly sanctuary (Hebrews 8:1-5; 1:3). Christ's ministry in the heavenly sanctuary was prefigured by the earthly sanctuary service, which was a shadow of the true (Hebrews 9:1-5)?

The earthly sanctuary service revealed the entire process of salvation. It revealed God's mercy, in providing for the sinner's atonement through the blood of the Lamb of God (represented by the animal sacrifices). It also revealed God's justice in the sense that sin must meet its punishment. Symbolically, the blood of the animal victims was accepted instead of the blood of the repentant sinner. The earthly sanctuary also revealed the active ministry that Jesus entered upon after His atoning death and resurrection on man's behalf—represented in the work of the earthly high priest. The priest had a daily round of services to offer, in the morning and evening sacrifices (referred to as the daily sacrifices), the burning of incense on the altar, the lighting of the candles and other services such as taking the blood of the animal sacrifices and applying it in the first apartment of the sanctuary. This represents the fact that since Christ's ascension, through His ministry as our Mediator and High Priest, the merits of His sacrifice have been constantly made available to all who are willing to exercise faith in Him. Man can enjoy a personal and intimate relationship with God because of Christ's mediatorial work.

Through its yearly service—the day of Atonement—the sanctuary also revealed the work of the investigative judgment that Christ will accomplish before His Second Coming to the earth to reward His saints. The service revealed that the mediatory work of Jesus in extending His merits to man and offering him salvation is not forever—God will one day put an end to sin (Leviticus 16). As once per year, the high priest would cleanse the sanctuary and the people of God from all their sins before the Lord, Jesus will one day complete the work of cleansing the heavenly sanctuary with His blood. The end of this service will symbolize the close of probation.

According to Ellen G. White, "The subject of the sanctuary and the investigative judgment should be clearly understood by the people of God. All need knowledge for themselves of the position and work of their High Priest. Otherwise, it will be impossible for them to exercise the faith which is essential at this time or to occupy the position which God designs them to fill"[12].

An understanding of the doctrine of the Sanctuary and Christ's ministry on our behalf should help to:

1. Assure us of the constant availability of God's grace and power even when we make mistakes (Hebrews 7:25; 1 John 2:1, 2).

2. Recognize the need to overcome every besetting sin, knowing that probation will soon close (Hebrews 12:1-2; Revelation 22:11, 12).

There are only a few of the basic doctrines that are necessary to establish and maintain a firm faith in Christ. For an extensive exposition for other fundamental teachings of Scripture, see *Seventh-day Adventist Believe.*

Those who are uncertain or waver in their faith and understanding of these and other fundamental truths of the Bible will continually fall into sin and need again and again to be taught the basic principles of repentance towards God and forgiveness of sins (Hebrews 5:12-6:3; Ephesians 4:11-16). Therefore, for spiritual maturity to exists, there must be a firm; unwavering understanding of and confidence in the fundamental teachings of the Bible.

---

[1] Ellen G. White, *Steps to Christ*, 9.

[2] Ellen G. White, *Patriarchs and Prophets* (Miami, Florida: Inter-American Division Publishing Association, 2002), 33.

[3] Ellen G. White, *Steps to Christ*, 11.

[4] Ibid, 12.

[5] Ellen G. White, *The Ministry of Healing* (EGW Writings Online: Ellen G. White Estate, Inc, 1905), 179.

[6] Ellen G. White, "Lowliness and Godly Sorrow". *Signs of the Times*, 1834.

[7] Anonymous, *The Kneeling Christian (Kindle Edition)* (The Fig Classic Series,

2012), 59.

[8] General Conference of Seventh-day Adventists, *Seventh-day Adventists Believe* (Boise, ID: Pacific Press Publishing Association, 2005), 119

[9] Ibid, 119.

[10] Ellen G. White, *The Great Controversy* (EGW Writings Online: Ellen G. White Estate, Inc, 1911), 72.

[11] Ibid, 72.

[12] Ibid, 488.

CHAPTER 6
How We Become Mature

We enter the Christian life by being "born again"; we become mature by "growing up into . . . . Christ" (Ephesians 4:15, see also 1 Peter 2:1, 2).

How does growth take place? Just as you were born again—we "grow in grace and in the knowledge of our Lord and Savior Jesus Christ" (2 Peter 3:18; Ephesians 2:8, 9).

How do we grow in grace? We grow in grace when you abide in and live our lives by faith in Christ (John 15:1-5).

How do we abide in Christ? We abide in Christ by exercising constant faith in His mercy as we walk in obedience to His word. If we are to remain Christians or become mature in Christ, we are to keep exercising the same faith in God's power (grace) that saved us. Once we do this, God's power will work in us to will and to do of His good pleasure (Phil. 2:13; 1:6).

Growth in the physical world is a miracle that is produced by a life that comes from God. "Consider the lilies of the field, how they grow," Jesus said, "they toil not, neither do they spin: And yet I say unto you, that even Solomon in all his glory was not arrayed like one of these" (Matthew 6:28, 29). God promises to bless us with spiritual growth just as He does for the lilies—they grow by constantly drawing from the resources that God provides for their growth. For our spiritual growth, you must do the same thing— receive our life and spiritual resources from Jesus (see Ephesians 1:3). The plant needs soil, water, air, sunlight, and proper care to grow healthy and strong. So, the Christian grows by the Word of God, the Holy Spirit, prayer, constant obedience, faithfulness in the face of trials and temptations, witnessing and fellowship.

The Word of God provides the resources for growth

The spiritual resources that Jesus provides for our spiritual growth are found in His word. According to Ellen G. White, "The life of Christ that gives life to the world is in His word. It was by His word that Jesus healed disease and cast out demons; by His word He stilled the sea, and raised the dead; . . .The whole Bible is a manifestation of Christ, and the Saviour desired to fix the faith of His followers on the word. When His visible presence should be withdrawn, the word must be their source of power."[1]

That is why Peter encouraged the new Christians— "as newborn babes, desire the sincere milk of the word that ye may grow thereby" (1 Peter 2:2). To the Jews, Jesus said, "I am the living bread which came down from heaven: if any man eat of this bread, he shall live for ever: and the bread that I will give is my flesh, which I will give for the life of the world (John 6:51). You partake of the life of Christ by studying and obeying His word (John 6:63). As we live the life of Christ (in obedience to His word) His life becomes our own (Galatians 2:20).

That is why the Word of God is so important to the Christian. What food is to the body, the word of God is to us (Matthew 4:4). We should not only study the Bible every day, but we are to obey its precepts to grow. Every jot and tittle of God's word must be brought into our lives. It is usually said, and rightly so that we become what we eat. This principle is also true in the spiritual realm. Just as how the elements of food that you eat, by assimilation and digestion, eventually make up our tissues and organs; so, it is that, as we replace old habits with the principles of God's word, our life is built entirely by the word of God (Matthew 7:24, 25).

God gives us His word as a complete and infallible guide to forming a righteous character (2 Timothy 3:16, 17). The Word of God provides the spiritual food that we need to nurture us and help us to grow spiritually (1 Peter 2:1, 2). Therefore, it is our duty as Christians (especially those who have recently come to the faith) to study, understand and obey God's word. We should make it a lifelong work to develop and perfect ways and means of getting the most out of Bible Study.

Here are four (4) important means of getting the most out of the Bible:

1. Read it

2. Study it

3. Memorize it

4. Obey it

Read it every day

We should make it a goal to read the Bible every day prayerfully and to read all of it (Joshua 1:8; Psalm 1:1, 2). If we read three (3) chapters of the Bible each day and five (5) chapters on Sabbaths, we can complete the entire Bible in one (1) year. Reading the entire Bible will help us to become acquainted with the overall principles of the Bible and therefore we can put its stories and principles in their right context. Here are some guidelines on how to read the Bible:

a. Always begin Bible-reading with prayer.

b. Begin with books that are easier to understand. For example (Mark, Luke, Genesis, etc).

c. Understand how the books of the Bible are categorized (see Chart)

d. Use a version of the Bible that is as closest to modern English and is faithful to the original text as possible (e.g. *Authorized King James Version, New King James Version, Revised Standard Version*)

e. Do not 'rush' your Bible-reading. Read for understanding, not merely for accomplishing a reading goal.

f. Keep a daily journal of new insights, observations, and discoveries. Practice to write down all insights that come to your mind.

g. Use the morning hours or the time when your mind is most alert for Bible readings.

Study it diligently

To get a deeper understanding of Bible truths especially some difficult passages, we need to do more than reading; we need to take time to study the Bible. According to Ellen G. White, "We should carefully study the Bible, asking God for the aid of the Holy Spirit, that we may understand His word. We should take one verse, and concentrate the mind on the task of ascertaining the thought which God has put in that verse for us. We should dwell upon the thought until it becomes our own, and we know 'what saith the Lord.'"[2]

To study the Bible is to take one verse, chapter, story or topic; read, research and reflect on it until we understand the lessons that God wants us to learn from it. Here are some guidelines for studying a passage of Scripture:

1. Before zooming in on the passage, make sure to read the entire book of the Bible that the passage is a part of, to understand its context.

2. Identify the beginning and ending points of the story or passage of Scripture. Do not take it for granted that the chapter divisions provide a reliable means of determining

where a thought begin and end.

3. After you have identified the passage under consideration, then use the following steps to get the most out of it:

Observation:

a. Read the passage multiple times (even in different versions of the Bible) until you understand what it is 'saying'.

b. Use a *Concordance* to identify other Bible texts and passages that may shed more light on what the current passage is saying.

c. Use *Bible Dictionaries*, Maps and *Encyclopedias* to assist you in understanding unfamiliar words, places and cultures.

d. Ask the 'who, where, when, why and how' questions of the passage.

e. As much as possible, seek to 'get into the shoe' of persons in the passage. You can do so by choosing one character and try to see things from his/her perspective.

f. In your own words attempt to relate what the passage is saying.

g. If it is a story, try to draw a picture to portray what the passage is saying.

h. Give the passage a title that encapsulates what it is saying (of no more than five (5) words).

i. Make sure to write down all your observations, no matter how insignificant they may appear to you.

Interpretation:

The Observation stage is to find out what the passage 'says'; the Interpretation stage is to find out the spiritual meaning of what the passage says.

a. Write down all the insights that the Holy Spirit impress on your mind concerning what each thought in the passage means.

b. Make sure to discuss your conclusions with others and/or compare them with reputable Bible Commentaries (i.e. *Seventh-day Adventist Bible Commentary*).

c. Make sure that your interpretations do not contradict established teachings of the Bible (2 Peter 1:20).

Application:

The final stage of the study is the Application stage. After you have discovered what the passage says and what it means, you need to ask, 'how does it apply to me?' The Scripture was first originally addressed to people who lived in a different time and culture than ours. Bible study aims to understand the principle of what God was teaching His people in the past, to apply it to our lives today properly. Proper application of the Scripture depends heavily on the credibility of the observation and interpretation.

Memorize it

While it might be impractical to memorize the entire Bible, it is very important to memorize some key Bible texts and principles. The word of God is our main safeguard against temptations. That is why the Psalmist David declared, "Thy word have I hid in mine heart, that I might not sin against thee" (Psalm 119:11). It was because Jesus had the Scriptures memorized that He was able to resist the temptations of Satan (Matthew 4:1-11). Therefore, besides reading and studying the Bible, it is important to commit portions of Scriptures to memory.

"The mind must be restrained, and not allowed to wander. It should be trained to dwell upon the Scriptures, and upon noble, elevating themes. Portions of Scripture, even whole chapters, may be committed to memory, to be repeated when Satan comes in with his temptations."[3]

Here are a few guidelines concerning how to better memorize the Scripture:

1. Start small. Memorize one or two simple and well-known verses until you can go to those that are less known.

2. Use Scriptures that have special meaning to you. For example, based on the experience that you are going through, some Scriptures will mean more to you than others at that time.

3. Write down or print the text (s) on a piece of paper, take it with you and take time out during the day to review and practice reciting it.

4. Focus first on studying the meaning of the texts, then on regurgitating it word for word. In other words, make sure you understand what the text is saying before attempting to memorize it.

5. Take time to share the meaning of the text with others.

Obey its principles

The main objective of Bible Study is to get to understand the principles of God's word so that we can put them into practice in our lives. Therefore, the final and most important step in Bible Study is to obey the word of God. Obeying God's word involves replacing sinful practices in our lives with the principles of God's word. This is what it means to be "sanctified by the truth" (John 17:17).

Here are some guidelines concerning how we can best implement the principles of God's word in our lives:

1. Make sure the principle is clearly understood by you and is coherent with the entire Bible. Misinterpretation of Scripture can lead to malpractices and fanaticism in our Christian life (2 Peter 3:15, 16). Therefore, while some principles will be clear and easy to be understood, others

are not so clear and will need a diligent study (on your part) and consultation with the rest of the Bible and other Christians for clarification on its meaning.

2. Practice obeying all the principles of God's word that are revealed to you already. Greater spiritual light (understanding) will only come to those who are obeying what is revealed to them (John 7:17; 12:35, 36).

3. Esteem the word of God above everything else, even above your present life. Count no sacrifice too great to make to conform your life to the principles of God's word (Job 23:12; Matthew 16:24, 25).

4. Even if you make mistakes, do not compromise on principle, continue to set high standards for yourself and ask God to help you to obey Him completely. "Whatever is to be done at His command may be accomplished in His strength. All His biddings are enablings."[4]

5. Remember, obeying God's word is the only way to truly prove that you love and have faith in Him (Luke 6:46-48).

The Holy Spirit keeps us alive Spiritually

To us, Jesus is not only the "Bread of Life" He is also the "Living Water." Of this fountain, we must drink for us to have life in us (John 4:14). Bread represents God's word; water, here represents the Holy Spirit, Whom God gives to all who believe in Jesus for spiritual life and power (John 7:37). Without the Holy Spirit, no spiritual birth or growth would take place in our lives (John 3:6; Romans 8:9). The Holy Spirit is the One responsible for giving us the life that Jesus died to give—He is the One who "works in us to will and to do of His good pleasure" (Phil. 2:13). The work of the Holy Spirit is closely aligned to God's word, for it is the Holy Spirit who inspired the holy men of God who wrote the Bible (2 Peter 1:20, 21).

To us, the Holy Spirit brings spiritual life, light, power, and guidance. Before His departure from this earth, Jesus spent a lot of time and effort, teaching the disciples about the importance of the work of the Holy Spirit. Though He would be invisible to the disciples; they were to pray for and accept the presence of the Holy Spirit by faith. He was to be an abiding Guest in their heart to guide and teach them as Jesus would. In obeying God's word, we obey the voice of the Holy Spirit, and the presence of the Holy Spirit helps us to understand more of God's word. In giving us the Holy Spirit, Jesus made certain that, at His departure, His followers would not be left as spiritual orphans. We have Someone to guide, to encourage and to lead us in the path that Jesus would—the "Comforter" or the "Spirit of truth" (John 16:13-16).

According to the word of God, if we are to grow spiritually, we ought to have the following attitude towards the Holy Spirit:

1. Receive Him into your heart by faith (John 14:16-18; Romans 8:9).

2. Listen to His voice (Revelation 2:7).

3. Obey His voice (Romans 8:14).

4. Do not grieve Him or persistently resist His pleadings (Eph. 4:30; Hebrews 3:7, 8; Matthew 12:31, 32).

5. Pray earnestly for His presence with you every day (Acts 1:6-8; Luke 11:9-13).

Prayer Keeps us Connected

If the Word of God represents food in our spiritual life; Prayer is to our spiritual life what breathing is to us physically. It is not breathing that keeps us alive; it's the air that we breathe. If we do not utilize the air through breathing, we will eventually die. So, it is with prayer. The power of God that keeps us alive and helps us to grow spiritually has been provided for us in abundance and more than we can ever ask for (2 Peter 1:3; Ephesians 3:20). However, if we do not ask for and thus receive power, we will have no life in us (Matthew 7:7-11; Acts 1:6-8).

Prayer helps us to partake of God's grace and power that He has made available to us through Jesus Christ (Hebrews 4:14-16). "Prayer is the key in the hand of faith to unlock heaven's storehouse."[5] Because we are constantly in need of God's blessings; the word of God encourages us to "pray without ceasing" (1 Thess. 5:17; see also Luke 18:1, 2). This does not mean that we are to be on our knees in prayer constantly, but that we are to maintain an unbroken connection with God by faith. For "without unceasing prayer and diligent watching we are in danger of growing careless and of deviating from the right path."[6]

Through prayer, we make provision for God to bestow upon us the blessings and strength that we need for spiritual growth. The power of the Holy Spirit (see Luke 11:9-13); Wisdom to overcome temptation and to do God's work (James 1:5; Matthew 6:9-11); Intimacy with God (James 4:8, 9); Forgiveness for sins and the cleansing power of the Holy Spirit (Psalm 51). In other words, prayer is how we receive all that God has provided for us and to give Him ourselves as He asked.

Why pray when God already knows?

1. Prayer helps us to develop and maintain a good *relationship* with God. Without communication, a relationship would die for lack of intimacy. Prayer helps us to be intimate with God as we share our deepest thoughts, needs, and feelings with Him.

2. Prayer is how we *ask for and receive strength* and blessings from God. "It is part of God's plan to grant us in answer to the prayer of faith, that which He would not bestow if we did not thus ask."[7]

3. Prayer helps us to *defeat temptation* when we call upon God for help. The battles that we must fight in the

Christian pathway are greater than we can handle in our own strength. Therefore, we need to pray—we need to pray for power to overcome temptation and to do God's will.

4. Prayer helps us to *maintain a continuous and unbroken connection with God.* Connection with God is essential to spiritual growth; prayer is the only means by which we can maintain a constant connection with God. Therefore, the Apostle Paul encourages us to "pray without ceasing" (1 Thessalonians 5:17).

5. It is through prayer that *we confess our sins* to God and *receive forgiveness* from Him.

What are some of the things we should pray for?

1. James 1:5 - Wisdom

2. Luke 11:13 – The Holy Spirit

3. Matthew 5:44 – Our Enemies

4. Matthew 6:11 – Our Daily Bread

5. Matthew 6:13 – For God's guidance

6. Matthew 6:12 - Forgiveness for our sins

7. Matthew 6:10 – For God's kingdom to come

8. James 5:13, 14 – For the sick

Guidelines for effective prayer

Prayer is an important habit to develop as a Christian. To develop an effective prayer life, here are some guidelines that you need to follow.

Set aside specific time and place to pray.

While we are always to maintain a connection with God

through prayer, it is very important to set aside specific times and place for personal/secret prayer (Matthew 6:6). We need to have special moments, especially in the morning, when we pour out our hearts to God in prayer; laying our burdens at His feet and drawing strength from Him for our daily tasks (Psalm 5:1-3). Jesus, while He was on earth, had special moments when He would get away from the crowd to hold communion with His Father; we too need to develop such habits, if we are to live a victorious Christian life (Matthew 14:23; Mark 6:46; Luke 6:12).

Exercise faith

Simply, "believe that He [God] is, and [that] He is a rewarder of them that diligently seek Him" (Heb. 11:6 margin). Accepting God by faith means that we should acknowledge the unseen realities of God's presence and all that we are told about Him in His word (2 Corinthians 4:18). By faith we should see our prayers ascending up before God and His throne; we should see the angels (as ministering spirits) ready to do God's bidding in answer to our prayers; we should know that God does not only hear our prayers, but that every sincere prayer will receive an answer and we should trust God's love for us, knowing that He always knows what is best for us. "For the LORD God is a sun and shield: the LORD will give grace and glory: no good thing will he withhold from them that walk uprightly" (Psalm 84:11 see also Daniel 9:20-23; Revelation 8:4; 1 John 5:14, 15).

Penitence

We should always approach the throne of God with a sense of our great need for Him; acknowledging our helplessness and our unworthiness while trusting in His love and mercy (see Luke 18:9-14; Psalm 51).

Forgiveness

We should maintain a spirit of forgiveness towards others if we are to pray effectively. "For if ye forgive men their trespasses, your heavenly Father will also forgive you: But if ye forgive not men their trespasses, neither will your Father forgive your trespasses" (Matthew 6:14, 15). Jesus also taught that our duty regarding forgiveness goes beyond merely overlooking the wrongs that others have done to us, but also involves making definite efforts to bring about reconciliation with those who have anything against us. "Therefore", Jesus says, "if thou bring thy gift to the altar, and there rememberest that thy brother hath ought against thee; Leave there thy gift before the altar, and go thy way; first be reconciled to thy brother, and then come and offer thy gift" (Matthew 5:23, 24).

Do not cherish any known sins.

It is the Psalmist David who said, "If I regard iniquity in my heart, the Lord will not hear me" (Psalm 66:18; see also Proverbs 28:13). "If we cling to any known sin, the Lord will not hear us", for though the Lord is great in mercy and goodness, He 'will by no means clear the guilty.'"[8] We should not only confess our sins to God, as we approach His throne, but we should confess to those whom we may have caused hurt (James 5:16).

Perseverance in Prayer

Perseverance in prayer refers both to maintaining an unbroken connection with God through prayer and persistence in depending on God's favor (Luke 18:1-8). Perseverance means that we are not to allow apparent delays in answer to our prayers to cause us to waver in our seeking after and depending on God.

Definiteness

We should be very definite (specific) about what we are asking the Lord for in prayer. We should avoid being so vague that we cannot truly tell whether or when our prayers are answered. Though the Lord already knows what we need, we demonstrate true faith and dependence on Him whenever we request Him in a specific way as a child would to his/her parent (Matthew 7:7-11).

Plan what you are going to pray about

Some prayers will be spontaneous and flow most times easily when you have a special burden. But we can eliminate boredom, monotony and the possibility of wandering in our prayers if we reflect on and write down the things we are going to pray about before we pray.

Develop and use various patterns of prayer

Even your prayer life can become monotonous if you do not take the time and effort needed to make it exciting and meaningful. The model prayer given by Jesus to His disciples is a good pattern to adopt in your prayers to give it a sense of purpose and direction.

Don't become a hermit

Prayer should not be independent of a life of active labour for God and service to others. As Ellen White suggests, "he who does nothing but pray will soon cease to pray, or his prayers will become a formal routine."[9] Based on what Jesus taught, the central focus of prayer should be the advancing of the purposes of God's kingdom on earth. And the best way to be intelligent in praying for God's kingdom to come and His will to be done on earth as in heaven is to be actively involved in carrying out God's will on earth.

Maintain an attitude of thanksgiving and praise to God

When we make it a habit to be grateful for God's blessings and provision in our lives; our faith will grow stronger. We would have fewer things to complain about and would be able to trust God more freely during difficult times if we practice taking note of and praise God for His goodness towards us. "Bless the LORD, O my soul, and *forget not* all his benefits:" the Psalmist declared (Psalm 103:2 emphasis supplied). It is good that when we approach God in prayer, we do not only have requests to make of Him, but we reflect on His goodness towards us.

Trials keep us humble

One of the most difficult experiences that I have faced as a Christian was one that took place in my early years as a pastor. After one year and a few months into my ministerial internship, due to a disagreement with my Conference President, I was dismissed from my job. To be fair to the persons involved, I will not discuss the circumstances surrounding the dismissal.

This was the first time in my Christian experience that I found myself praying about a situation that would not go away. My practice was that if I faced a challenging situation, I knew that once I spent a few moments with God in prayer, I would feel better about the situation, or God would work out something.

However, from the day I collected my dismissal letter to a few months after "prayer didn't work" as it used to. Whenever I prayed, it felt like heaven was empty. Even my morning devotions (which would be my best times for prayer) felt like a mere routine. I would pray for hours; yet get up and felt the same way. I would read the Bible, but I would not get that satisfying feeling and assurance that God was with me. During those times, Job 23 became my favorite passage of Scripture.

Job said,
"Oh, that I knew where I might find him,
that I might come even to his seat!

I would lay my case before him
and fill my mouth with arguments.

I would know what he would answer me
and understand what he would say to me.

Would he contend with me in the greatness of his power?

No; he would pay attention to me.

There an upright man could argue with him,
and I would be acquitted forever by my judge.

"Behold, I go forward, but he is not there,
and backward, but I do not perceive him;

on the left hand when he is working, I do not behold him;
he turns to the right hand, but I do not see him."
(Job 23:3-9, ESV).

Job laments that he cannot "find God" when he goes to his usual meeting places. That's how I felt. I felt like there was this weight on me that would not go away. I felt like there was a disconnect between myself and God, yet prayer and Bible study appeared not to be fixing it.

Trials and temptations are what makes the Christian experience difficult. Paraphrasing what the author of the book *The Kneeling Christian* (Anonymous 2012) said earlier about prayer, I would say, "If there were no Devil, the Christian experience would be an easy one."[10]

Trials come in many forms--persecution, sickness, loss of loved ones (through death or broken relationships), loss of income, loss of personal property and much more. Anything that challenges our faith in a way that causes us to think about giving up is a trial. For the Christian, trials are unavoidable and most times unexpected. Despite all of this, trials provide the greatest opportunities for us to grow as Christians. We need to have the right attitude towards them.

Understanding Trials

Here, I would like to share some things about trials that we need to understand.

Trials are part of God's plan to help us grow

According to Ellen G. White, "Trials and obstacles are the Lord's chosen methods of discipline and His appointed conditions of success."[11]

In other words, the endurance of trials helps us to be better Christians. When we endure trials, we allow God's purposes for the trial to be accomplished in us. When faced with trials, we will feel vulnerable and helpless. However, trials provide great opportunities to trust in God and prove our dependence on Him. We will not understand what is happening, but, like Job, we should trust the results to God.

The secret to how trials help us to grow is that without trials it is very difficult to tell where we are in our experience with God. Trials help to reveal what is lacking in our faith so that we can pray for the wisdom we need to perfect our faith (James 1:5-7). As the Apostle James said, "Count it all joy, my brothers, when you meet trials of various kinds, for you know that the testing of your faith produces steadfastness. And let steadfastness have its full effect, that you may be perfect and complete, lacking in nothing" (James 1:1-4, ESV).

Trials evoke the deepest emotions and inspirations

The experience of enduring trials is a great source of inspiration because through trials we see the power of God in our lives as never before. Because, through trials, we are forced to depend on God as never before. Israel saw His glory manifested against Egypt on their behalf and during the trying wilderness experience, they saw God's glory provide for and protect them (Hebrews 4; Deut. 8).

It is because of seeing God's working through trying experiences that David wrote most of the Psalms. For example, Psalm 27, 34 and 91. Some of the most beautiful Hymns and Christian songs were written out of trying experiences. Most popular of which is the hymn, "When Peace Like a River", written by Horatio G. Spafford, who lost his four daughters through tragic circumstances. In the new earth, it is a reflection on God's deliverance that will inspire the song of Moses and the Lamb. For then, the veil is removed, and we can see more deeply the wonderful workings of God in our behalf, even in situations where we thought He wasn't.

Trials prepare us to help others

Thirdly, trials provide the experience we need to be a source of strength to others who face similar trials to ours. According to the Apostle Paul, "Blessed be the God and Father of our Lord Jesus Christ, the Father of mercies and God of all comfort, who comforts us in all our affliction, so that we may be able to comfort those who are in any affliction, with the comfort with which we ourselves are comforted by God" (2 Corinthians 1:3-4, ESV).

"When you are converted, strengthen your brethren," Jesus told Peter (Luke 22:32). And after the experience of the cross, Jesus made sure to charge him, "feed My lambs and My sheep." Jesus knew that through the trying experiences of the cross, Peter could be a source of inspiration and strength to other believers. Later, Peter was able to encourage the believers, "Beloved, do not be surprised at the fiery trial when it comes upon you to test you, as though something strange were happening to you." (1 Peter 4:12, ESV).

We will never face a trial that is beyond our ability to endure

Despite its unpredictable nature trials are still under God's control. We may not have expected them, but God sees and weighs trials before they come to us. And He promised that He would never allow us to be tempted more than we can bear (1 Corinthians 10:13). We get firsthand knowledge of this in the experience of Job. Satan was not permitted to go beyond what God's word allowed (Job 1:12).

We may have to live with some trials all our lives

Some trials will be overcome only by experiencing a new norm. When the Apostle Paul asked God three times to remove the "thorn in his flesh," he was told no (2 Corinthians 12). In other words, he (Paul) would have to live with it. When our son was diagnosed with sickle cell disease, my wife and I were disappointed, but very optimistic. We hoped that change would come. However, after a few hospitalizations, we eventually accepted the fact that despite our prayers and best effort, hospitalization and pain might be a permanent part of our lives, especially our son's. Well known hymn writer, Fanny Crosby, who became blind at three months due to the negligence of a physician, remained blind all her life.

We can lose the blessing of trials

Finally, we must understand that we can lose the blessing of trials if we fail to endure. We observe this in the experience of the children of Israel in the wilderness. They all "passed through the cloud", they all drank of that spiritual Rock, but they did not all benefit, because of unbelief the Apostle Paul said (1 Corinthians 10:1-5; Hebrews 4). According to Ellen G. White "If we overcome our trials and get victory over the temptations of Satan, then we endure the trial of our faith, which is more precious than gold, and are stronger and better prepared to meet the next. But if we sink down and give way to the temptations of Satan, we shall grow weaker and get no reward for the trial and shall not be so well prepared for the next. In this way we shall grow weaker and weaker, until we are led captive by Satan at his will."[12]

According to the Apostle James, a blessing is promised only to those who endure, "Blessed is the man who remains steadfast under trial, for when he has stood the test, he will receive the crown of life, which God has promised to those who love him" (James 1:12). Countless times, the Bible makes it clear that ultimately the blessing of salvation belong to those who "endure to the end" (Matthew 24:13).

How to Overcome Trials

In the following section, I share a few guidelines for overcoming and reaping the true benefits of trials.

Be prepared

It's hard to prepare for something we can't predict. But that's a hallmark of the Christian experience—to be always ready. We prepare ourselves by maintaining a consistent relationship with God through prayer, Bible study, and obedience. The parable of the two men who built their houses represents those who were prepared and those who were not.

Keep the connection line

During the trial, as far as possible, do not give up your routine of Bible study and prayer. Some trials will physically displace us. The temptation in these situations is to "go with the flow" of allowing inconvenience to deprive us of well-needed help from God. However, during the trial, is when we need Him the most. "Couldn't you pray with Me for 1 hour", said Jesus to the disciples. Jesus knew the importance of prayer in helping us to endure trial. Therefore, He urged the disciples to pray, despite their weariness.

Take notes

Take note of and pray about any weaknesses or shortcomings that this trial may bring to your attention. God uses trials to help us understand ourselves better. According to the Apostle James, trials should produce steadfastness in us. However, "If any of you lacks wisdom, let him ask God, who gives generously to all without reproach, and it will be given him" (James 1:5, ESV). In other words, God will bless us with all the wisdom we need to overcome our weaknesses.

Do not give up on God even if you make mistakes

Jesus knew that Peter's faith would have been severely tried during His arrest and crucifixion. Therefore, Jesus prayed that Peter would repent of his sins and learn from his mistakes. "Simon, Simon, behold, Satan demanded to have you, that he might sift you like wheat, but I have prayed for you that your faith may not fail. And when you have turned again, strengthen your brothers" (Luke 22:31-32).

Praise and Thanksgiving

Remind yourself of God's goodness, kindness and power. During a trial it is very easy to forget these things. Praising God; focusing on His greatness; His love and power is the greatest antidote to depressed and discouraging feelings. Here are some important reasons we need to praise God and be thankful during a trial:

1. It could be worse. Many are facing worse than you. Give thanks for any privileges you still possess.

2. God is still in control.

3. God is still good.

4. God cares for you.

5. God is always present.

Do not forget to say thanks to God when He takes you through trying circumstances.

Keep the end in mind

Finally, to overcome trials, we need to focus on the glorious end that God has in mind; not only for this life, but the life to come. "Count it all joy, my brothers, when you meet trials of various kinds", the Apostle James said, "for you know that the testing of your faith produces steadfastness" (James 1:2-3, ESV). The Apostle Paul said that our "light momentary affliction is preparing for us an eternal weight of glory beyond all comparison, as we look not to the things that are seen but to the things that are unseen. For the things that are seen are transient, but the things that are unseen are eternal" (2 Corinthians 4:17-18).

Temptation keeps us vigilant

Temptation means enticement to sin. Temptation is like trials. Matter of fact, it could be said that temptation is a trial. The only difference is that, according to the Bible, God doesn't tempt us (James 1:12). We are tempted when we are drawn away after our lust. It could be said that trials are based on outward circumstances, temptations; inward desires.

Temptation also provides an opportunity for us to grow spiritually. Rick Waren gives some excellent tips for overcoming temptation[13]. Here, I will share a few of them:

Do not become *discouraged* or *frightened* by temptation.

To be tempted is not a sin; we sin when we yield to temptation and choose to disobey God. Satan cannot force us to disobey God. He can tempt, harass, annoy and accuse, but he cannot force us to go against God's will. Before we sin, we must choose to disobey God. Satan makes evil suggestions, but that is as far as he can go; he cannot force us to sin. Therefore, there is no need to become discouraged whenever evil thoughts pop-up in your heads.

Maintain a constant devotional life.

We should fortify our minds with the word of God and prayer so that we do not become easy prey to Satan's temptations (Psalm 119:11; Ephesians 6:10-12). By not maintaining a strong connection with God through prayer and the study of the word, we make ourselves twice vulnerable to the attacks of Satan. According to Ellen G. White, "The darkness of the evil one encloses those who neglect to pray. The whispered temptations of the enemy entice them to sin; and it is all because they do not make use of the privileges that God has given them in the divine appointment of prayer."[14] She also said, if we "Neglect the exercise of prayer, or engage in prayer spasmodically, now and then, as seems convenient, and you lose your hold on God. The spiritual faculties lose their vitality, the religious experience lacks health and vigor."[15]

Recognize the vulnerable situations and circumstances

For example, if you were an alcoholic, then you know that you have a weakness for alcohol. Therefore, it would not be wise to constantly be around friends who are drinking, for the mere sake of having fun. "We are not to place ourselves needlessly in the way of temptation. God says, "Come out from among them, and be ye separate, ... and touch not the unclean thing; and I will receive you, and will be a Father unto you, and ye shall be My sons and daughters." If by associating with worldlings for pleasure, by conforming to worldly practices, by uniting our interests with unbelievers, we place our feet in the path of temptation and sin, how can we expect God to keep us from falling? . . . . . Keep yourselves away from the corrupting influences of the world. Do not go unbidden to places where the forces of the enemy are strongly entrenched."[16]

Seek God's help

God wants us to call on Him in times of temptation. We are no match for the Devil. Therefore, we always need God's help to overcome. When we face temptation, we can call upon God with silent prayers, having the assurance that God hears and will help us to overcome (Hebrews 4:14-16). Sometimes we are embarrassed to ask God for help because we feel guilty to be falling into temptation repeatedly. But God never gets weary of helping us.

Recognize that there is always *a way out* (1 Corinthians 10:13).

In every time of temptation, God always provides a way of escape. We must believe God's promises and claim them by choosing to depend on God and not give in to temptation. No matter how great temptation may appear, God will not allow you to be tempted more than you can bear in His strength. In other words, there is never an excuse for giving in to temptation. If we choose to depend on God, Satan cannot overcome us.

Refocus your attention on godly thoughts

We should resist the devil, but not try to resist temptation. Each time you try to block a thought out of your mind, you drive it deeper into your memory. By resisting it, you reinforce it. The battle for sin is won or lost in your mind. Whatever gets your attention will get you. We get rid of thought by focusing on something else. Sing a spiritual song; meditate on a passage of Scripture; just focus your mind on things that are spiritual; therefore, there will be no space for evil thoughts (Philippians 4:8; Colossians 3:1, 2; Ephesians 5:19). These things help us to draw near to God (James 4:7, 8). "We should accustom ourselves to often lift the thoughts to God in prayer. If the mind wanders, we must bring it back; by persevering effort, habit will finally make it easy. We cannot for one moment separate ourselves from Christ with safety."[17]

Realize your vulnerability

Given the right situation, any of us are capable of any sin. Therefore, no matter how many victories we have had, we must never let down our guard and think we are beyond temptation (1 Corinthians 10:12). "We cannot keep ourselves from sin for one moment. Every moment we are dependent upon God."[18]

Therefore, "Those who have felt the sanctifying and transforming power of God, must not fall into the dangerous error of thinking that they are sinless, that they have reached the highest state of perfection, and are beyond the reach of temptation."[19]

Witnessing keeps us on the cutting edge

We share our faith with others to help them to know the Lord (Matthew 28:18-20). While we are on this earth, this is the work that God has appointed us—to make disciples of other men (Acts 1:8). All other work is to be made subordinate to this one. God blesses us with salvation, with the power of the Holy Spirit, with wisdom, with spiritual gifts, not only for us to grow up in Christ, but for us to join Him in being a blessing to others; to help change their lives.

This important exercise of sharing our faith with others is not only a natural desire of those who are born again; it is also necessary and beneficial to spiritual growth. When we share our faith with others, our faith grows and become stronger. I have found, in my own experience, that the very words that I use to encourage others are words that come back to me, to encourage me in times of difficulty.

By testifying to others about God, we make ourselves channels of His grace. And if God's grace is flowing through us daily, we can only be blessed and enriched by doing so. To neglect this experience would be to us spiritually what neglecting physical exercise is to our body--our faith would become fossilized.

I have also found that the more we share our faith with others, the greater will be our capacity and desire to know God.

Here are a few important things that witnessing does to help strengthen our spiritual life:

1. It keeps us in tune with God's passion. God's passion is people. When we realize and keep before our minds how passionate God is about people, we cannot help but understand how passionate He is about us.

2. It gives fuel and meaning to our prayer life.

3. It broadens our understanding of the Bible and deepens our capacity to know more.

Steps to becoming an effective witness for Christ

Witnessing can be daunting if you do not know where to start. Therefore, I would like to share a brief overview of the steps to becoming an effective witness for Christ. These are general principles that apply to you despite your area of giftedness and interest.

Be converted

We cannot effectively bear witness about the power of the gospel unless we have felt its power in our lives. Those who have felt the sanctifying power of the gospel, sharing its message will be a pleasure and a natural desire. According to Ellen G. White, "No sooner does one come to Christ than there is born in his heart a desire to make known to others what a precious friend he has found in Jesus; the saving and sanctifying truth cannot be shut up in his heart."[20]

Know your area of giftedness

We should all seek to understand the witnessing methods that we are best adapted to, based on our personality, talents, and gifts. Once we know this, we should improve and capitalize on these talents for the glory of God. God has appointed not only every man his work, but also spiritual gifts, talents, and abilities to accomplish this work. The more we understand ourselves, the better we can take advantage of opportunities to witness.

Know the Bible

The Apostle Peter declares "...sanctify the Lord God in your hearts: and be ready always to give an answer to every man that asketh you a reason of the hope that is in you with meekness and fear:" (1 Peter 3:15). To be always ready to give a reason for our faith, we need to have a clear understanding of what the Bible teaches and how it relates to the gospel (2 Timothy 2:15). We should be able, like Phillip, to begin from one passage of Scripture and "preach Jesus" with conviction and authority (Acts 8:35). This we can accomplish only by systematically studying the entire Bible and getting to understand its principles by practically applying them to our lives each day (John 7:17).

Seek training

"We must not enter into the Lord's work haphazard and expect success", says Ellen G. White, " . . . . Jesus calls for co-workers, not blunderers . . . . Mechanics, lawyers, merchants, men of all trades and professions, educate themselves that they may become masters of their business. Should the follower of Christ be less intelligent, and while professedly engaged in His service be ignorant of the ways and means to be employed? The enterprise of gaining everlasting life is above every earthly consideration."[21] Equip yourself in various methods of witnessing and approaches to witnessing. You can do this by attending witnessing workshops, watch online videos, reading or attend seminary. Whatever method you choose, it is important that you take advantage of the wealth of knowledge available from experienced and successful evangelists.

Use Christ's Method of Witnessing

Before approaching anyone about the gospel, we should study how to meet people where they are. As the popular saying goes, "no one cares how much you know, until they know how much you care." A person's standing with God is a personal and intimate matter; no one will feel comfortable discussing such intimate details of their lives with you, unless they learn to trust you. That is why. Ellen G. White says that, "Christ's method alone will give true success in reaching the people. The Saviour mingled with men as one who desired their good. He showed His sympathy for them, ministered to their needs and won their confidence. Then He bade them, 'Come, follow Me.'"[22]

Start witnessing to those next to you

Your widest and most flourishing field for witnessing activities, is usually found next to you—in your home, neighborhood, at your workplace and school environments. In these areas, you'll find people with whom you already have friendships and who have confidence in you. These are the people over whose lives you have the greatest influence. Therefore, it takes less time and effort to relate the gospel message to them in a way that they would understand. My first witnessing activity after I was converted was to establish regular worship in my home. My next field of labour was to start a short devotion with my co-workers. These may appear to be simple tasks, but they were the training ground that helped to prepare me for a life of public ministry.

Utilize the power of prayer in our witnessing

We should not underestimate the power of intercessory prayer. Only the Holy Spirit can bring about conviction and conversion in people's lives. Therefore, before we speak to men about God, we should first speak to God about men. Ask for the help of the Holy Spirit and for wisdom to reach each heart. Remember, God knows the people we are witnessing to more than we do. He knows where they are and what they need to hear. We should pray for God to grant us wisdom to approach people, based on what He knows about them. Thus, though the person might not decide immediately, our witness would have been effective, because it was done in harmony with God's program. According to Ellen G. White, "It is not the power that emanates from men that makes the work successful, it is the power of the heavenly intelligences working with the human agent that brings the work to perfection.

A Paul may plant, and an Apollos may water, but it is God that giveth the increase. Man cannot do God's part of the work. As a human agent he may cooperate with the divine intelligences, and in simplicity and meekness do his best, realizing that God is the great Master Work-man."[23]

Possess a meek spirit

To be a witness for Jesus is to be a soldier in Christ army who is constantly engaged in conflict. It is a sure thing, that though we are called upon to approach everyone in a friendly manner, that we will not always get a friendly response. However, the Bible teaches us that "...the servant of the Lord must not strive; but be gentle unto all men, apt to teach, patient, In meekness instructing those that oppose themselves; if God peradventure will give them repentance to the acknowledging of the truth; And that they may recover themselves out of the snare of the devil, who are taken captive by him at his will" (2 Timothy 2:24-26). Also, while we are called upon to meet every argument with solid Bible-based response, we should try our best to avoid, "foolish and unlearned questions . . . ., knowing that they do gender strifes" (2 Timothy 2:23). Sometimes, we can win an argument, but lose a friend. We need to be sensitive enough to know when to pursue an argument and when not to. People, who are genuinely seeking for truth, will ask questions of our faith that will produce wonderful discussions. However, there are persons who ask question for no profit, but to (as Paul says) engender strife. These we should try our best to avoid.

Growing together

The word 'fellowship' from the Greek word, 'konoinia,' which means, "fellowship with or participation in anything; a communion, fellowship, society."[24] This word played a very important role in the development of the vocabulary of the early church. From this word, we derive community, communion, and fellowship. When we are 'born again', we are born into a family/community. This family is God's church--the community of believers (Acts 2:47).

The greatest thing about being part of this fellowship is that we are not only joined to each other, but to the Lord. "That which we have seen" said the Apostle John, "and heard we declare to you, that you also may have fellowship with us; and truly our fellowship is with the Father and with His Son Jesus Christ" (1 John 3:3). In helping the Apostles to grow up and become mature Christians, Jesus did not only provide for their contact and fellowship with Him, He also made provision for them to have personal contact with each other.

He brought these men together, from different backgrounds, experience, and temperament and told them, "A new commandment I give to you, that you love one another; as I have loved you, that you also love one another. By this shall all men know that you are My disciples, if you have love for one another" (John 13:34, 35 NKJV).

Jesus knew that the greatest demonstration of His power to save from sin and of the gospel is its power to change people from selfishness to being loving. By the power of this love, His disciples (though different in so many ways) would become "one" as He and the Father are "one" (John 17:21-23). This is where the rubber meets the road--that by the gospel--men, who are (by nature) sinful and selfish, would be brought together into a community of love. A community of which it could be said, they were of "one heart and one soul" (Acts 4:32).

Here is what fellowship is all about—living in or being a part of God's family. Some persons advocate individual accountability to God above accountability to the community of faith (the church). It appears they want to be 'accountable to God', but not to the community of faith. According to the Apostle John, it is impossible to claim that we are Christians, while we neglect our obligation to our brothers in Christ. "If a man says, I love God, and hateth his brother, he is a liar: for he that loveth not his brother whom he hath seen, how can he love God whom he hath not seen?" (1 John 4:20).

Fellowship is important to the Christian life and growth, not only because of what it requires but the blessings that it brings. Two of the main blessings that the fellowship provides are mentorship and support.

Mentorship

Jesus expected that the type of leadership and mentorship that He provided for His disciples while He was with them on the earth, would be replicated in the church. Jesus was an example to the flock. What He wanted them to be, in life and ministry, He was. He bore long with their shortcomings and took time out to teach, train and encouraged them in their labours. This is what Jesus expected of those who have benefited from following Him to do—to make disciples of and to mentor those who are young in the flock.

That is why, before His crucifixion and Peter's denial of Him, Jesus said to Peter, "Simon, Simon, behold, Satan hath desired to have you, that he may sift you as wheat: But I have prayed for thee, that thy faith fail not: *and when thou art converted, strengthen thy brethren*" (Luke 22:32 emphasis supplied). After His resurrection, and after giving Peter the opportunity to reaffirm his love for his Lord, Jesus commissioned Peter, as He does to the other disciples, "Feed My sheep/lambs" (see John 21:15-17). Peter himself, admonished the elders in one church to do the same thing—"Feed the flock of God which is among you, taking the oversight thereof, not by constraint, but willingly; not for filthy lucre, but of a ready mind; Neither as being lords over God's heritage, but being ensamples to the flock" (1 Peter 5:2-3). Therefore, being a member of God's church on earth helps us to grow spiritually, in that we get to learn from the instructions and godly example of those who are more experienced in the things of God than we are.

Support

As I have said before, the Christian experience is a challenging one, and it is even made more challenging if we attempt to walk it on our own. According to the wise man Solomon, "Two are better than one; because they have a good reward for their labour. For if they fall, the one will lift up his fellow: but woe to him that is alone when he falleth; for he hath not another to help him up . . . . And if one prevail against him, two shall withstand him; and a threefold cord is not quickly broken" (Ecclesiastes 4:9-12). Being part of God's Church provides the opportunity to find encouragement and support to continue our walk even in the face of discouragement.

Conclusion

God has provided all the resources we need for spiritual growth. The word of God, prayer, the Holy Spirit, a spiritual community (the church) and the call to Service. These spiritual disciplines are indispensable to spiritual growth.

---

[1] Ellen G. White, *The Desire of Ages* (EGW Writings Online: Ellen G. White Estate, Inc, 1898), 390.

[2] Ibid, 390.

[3] Ellen G. White, *Our High Calling* (EGW Writings Online: Ellen G. White Estate, Inc, 1961), 88.

[4] Ellen G. White, *Christ's Object Lessons* (Review and Herald Publishing Association, 1900), 333.

[5] Ellen G. White, *Steps to Christ* (Pacific Press Publishing Association, 1892), 94.

[6] Ibid, 95.

[7] Ellen G. White, *The Great Controversy*, 525.

[8] Ellen G. White, *Steps to Christ*, 95.

[9] Ibid, 101.

[10] Anonymous, *The Kneeling Christian*, 59.

---

[11] Ellen G. White, *The Ministry of Healing* (EGW Writings Online: Ellen G. White Estate, Inc, 1905), 471.

[12] Ellen G. White, *Early Writings* (EGW Writings Online: Ellen G. White Estate, Inc, 1882), 46.

[13] Rick Waren, *Purpose-Driven Life* (Grand Rapids, Michigan: Zondervan, 2002), 203-206.

[14] Ellen G. White, *Steps to Christ*, 94.

[15] Ellen G. White, *Gospel Workers* (EGW Writings Online: Ellen G. White Estate, Inc, 1915), 254.

[16] Ellen G. White. *Messages to Young People* (Silver Spring, Maryland: Review and Herald Publishing Association, 1930), 82.

[17] Ibid, 82.

[18] Ellen G. White, *The Ministry of Healing*, 179

[19] Ellen G. White, *The Signs of the Times*, 1834.

[20] Ellen G. White, *Steps to Christ*, 78.

[21] Ellen G. White, *Christian Service* (EGW Writings Online: Ellen G. White Estate, Inc, 1925), 224.

[22] Ellen G. White, *The Ministry of Healing*, 143.

[23] Ellen G. White, *Christian Service*, 260.

[24] Spiros Zodhates, *Lexical Aids to the New Testament, Revised Edition*, 1730.

CHAPTER 7
Hindrances to Spiritual Growth

If success in the Christian life depends on our continuous connection with (abiding in) Christ; then our greatest threat is distraction. Distraction leads to disconnection.

Distraction refers to anything or anyone that leads us to loosen our dependence on Christ. We often blame a 'particular weakness' or temptation for our failures. However, those are only the fruits of distraction. As Ellen G. White suggests, we cannot keep ourselves from sin for even a moment without Christ[1]. But, in Christ, we are an impregnable fortress.

This principle came home to me very clearly through an experience I had while working in the Bay Islands of Honduras. The Bay Islands is a group of 3 small Islands off the coast of Honduras. I lived in the largest one (Roatan). To get on the mainland you travel either by plane or ferry. The first time I travelled to the mainland, I traveled via the ferry.

While boarding the ferry, I noticed a young lady was handing out paper bags to all the passengers. I did not know for what reason, and I did not see the need for it, so I didn't take any. Halfway the journey I started to regret my decision. I started to feel nauseous. Luckily, I did not throw up. I was able to make it through the 1 ½ hour journey without giving in to my seasickness.

On my way back, I met a friend (a tourist from Canada). I told him about my experience while coming. He explained to me what happened and gave me good advice. He said it was the "see-saw" movement of my eyes that caused the nauseous feeling. He said, once I can prevent my eyes from moving, I could prevent nausea. To do that, I need to find the horizon and fix my eyes on it. I did that, and it worked. At least for a while until I got distracted and forgot to keep my eyes on the horizon.

I learned a lesson that day about keeping my eyes on Jesus. I realize how big an issue distraction is. I learnt that I must do whatever it takes to keep my eyes on Jesus.

The parable of the "sower who went forth to sow" taught some important principles about what it takes to be successful and what prevents success.

In the parable, there are three groups of hearers—1) those who experienced no growth (those seeds that fell by the wayside); 2) those that experienced growth but did not experience maturity and 3) those that not only experienced growth but bore fruit to the glory of God.

I could easily have categorized them as those that got distracted and those that did not; those who were hindered and those who were not; those who bore fruit and those who did not.

As to the things that hinder a Christian from growing up, we could make up an infinite list. However, based on what Jesus taught in the parable, we can put them into two categories—1) "lack of earth" and 2) "the thorns."

"No Deepness of Earth"

In the parable of the sower, Jesus describes the experience of the seeds that fell on stony ground as follows, "Some fell upon stony places, where they had not much earth: and forthwith they sprung up, because they had no deepness of earth." The interpretation that Jesus gives for this is, "he that received the seed into stony places, the same is he that heareth the word, and anon with joy receiveth it; Yet hath he not root in himself, but dureth for a while: for when tribulation or persecution ariseth because of the word, by and by he is offended" (Matthew 13:5, 20, 21).

It is very easy (from a surface look at the parable) to conclude that it was the 'tribulation and persecution' that hindered the 'stony-ground' hearer. This not so. Tribulation and persecution are not unique to the 'stony-ground' hearers. The Bible tells us that all who attempt to live godly will face tribulation and persecution (2 Timothy 3:12). According to the Apostle Paul, "...we glory in tribulations" (Romans 5:3). As Jesus mentioned in the parable of those who hear His word and do it, (no matter the condition of the house [that represents our lives]) the floods will come, and the rains will beat. But whether we stand, or fall depends on the level of our experience with the Lord (see Matthew 7:24-29).

It is the spiritual experience of the 'stony-ground hearers' (or the lack thereof) that prevents them from growing up to bear fruit in the Lord. Their spiritual experience is described as "...they had not much earth"; "no deepness of earth"; "they had no root" (Matthew 13:5, 6). The word of God was not given enough space in their lives.

As discussed in the previous chapter, the word of God is to take root in the heart and bear fruit in the life. This means that the person's entire life is to be brought in harmony with the principles of God's word. The stones among which the seeds fell, represents selfishness and sin—which are opposing principles to God's word (Ezekiel 36:26, 27). The human heart is naturally selfish; full of stubbornness (Jeremiah. 17:9). Therefore, in preparing to receive the word, the "fallow ground" of one's heart, must be broken up (Jer. 4:3). The stones should be taken out and the thorns removed.

For healthy spiritual growth to take place in the believer's life, there must be a continual and ongoing process of turning from self to Christ. "If any man will come after Me" Jesus said, "let him deny himself, and take up his cross daily, and follow Me" (Luke

9:23 emphasis supplied). The human heart is naturally opposed to this life of self-denial, and utter dependence on God, but it is an indispensable discipline for those who would be successful Christians. We are not naturally disposed to everyday life of surrendering our lives to God, Bible study, prayer, be on guard against temptation, and suffering for the cause of Christ, but these things are important disciplines (Philippians 1:29; Romans 8:17).

Those who in this manner "lose their lives" for Christ sake "will find it" (Matthew 16:24, 25). In that, they will find themselves becoming unselfish and more like Christ each day. But, those who desire to save their lives (or let their selfish and self-sufficient ways remain) will lose it (Luke 9:24).

Here is the experience of the 'stony ground hearer.' He desires the life of Christ but scorns the practical application of the word of God to his life. Therefore, he has 'not much earth' or 'no root in himself'. He is like the man who builds his house upon the sand. He neglects a thorough devotional life and the things that promote spiritual growth. Therefore, his experience is superficial and rightly will not stand when tribulation comes.

Three things contribute to the 'stony ground hearers' downfall, neglect of devotional life, unwillingness to surrender to the word and lack of discipleship.

Neglect of devotional exercises

The stony-ground hearer's spiritual growth is hindered by a lack of commitment to the things that promote spiritual growth, such as bible study, prayer, fellowship, and witnessing. They read the bible, pray and attend church now and then, but does not consider these things an integral part of their lives. Therefore, their spiritual life will lack the stamina it needs to endure trials. According to Ellen G. White, If you "neglect the exercise of prayer, or engage in prayer spasmodically, now and then, as seems convenient, and you lose your hold on God. The spiritual faculties lose their vitality; the religious experience lacks health and vigor."[2]

Unwillingness to surrender to the word

'The stony ground hearer' represents those who are satisfied with an appearance of godliness—which usually consists merely of their initial experience with Christ (2 Timothy 3:5). They usually spend a lot of time talking about the wonderful experiences of the past, upon which they base their assurance of salvation. But, besides this, they do not make any special effort to develop Christian virtues or to give up their ways for Christ.

Lack of nurture or discipleship

Sometimes the 'lack of earth' is not to be entirely blamed on the part of the hearer. A lack of discipleship and nurture can help to prevent a Christian from getting the experience that he or she needs to grow up in the Lord. According to Keith M. Bailey, in his book *Care of Converts*, "The condition of prolonged spiritual infancy is, in most cases, the result of poor discipleship or no discipleship at all. Converts are no more able to care for themselves than babies can care for themselves. Neglect of the new convert at this stage tends to make him a spiritual dropout or it locks him into permanent babyhood."[3] If left on their own, a new Christian is more inclined to return to their former life than to continue in the Lord. Every born-again child of God needs a family with a strong mentorship to grow spiritually healthy. If this support is lacking, then so will be the environment in which healthy spiritual growth can take place.

"The Thorns"

The experience of the seeds that fell among thorns is slightly different from those that fell among rocky soil. Their problem, unlike the stony-ground hearers, is not a lack of earth, but the thorns that they allow to grow up in their lives.

Jesus described their experience as follows, "...some fell among thorns; and the thorns sprung up and choked them." He gave the interpretation: "He . . . . that received seed among thorns is he that heareth the word; and the care of this world, and the deceitfulness of riches, choke the word, and he becometh unfruitful" (Matthew 13:7, 22 emphases supplied).

Here is presented the experience of one who does grow spiritually; probably even more than the stony-ground hearer. Their problem, then, is not that they do not keep up a good devotional life or does not value these things. It is not that they do not have a genuine desire to grow in the Lord and to do His work. It's just that they are not careful enough to prevent the wrong things from growing in their lives. The problem with the stony-ground hearer is that there is not enough growth, but the problem with the thorny-ground hearer is that, along with the good seed, thorns can grow.

The thorns, here, represent sinful habits or cherished sins. This hearer's spiritual experience is eroded by an equally absorbing interest. Therefore, as Christ said, "No man can serve two masters: for either he will hate the one and love the other; or else he will hold to the one and despise the other." This hearer eventually holds to the sins that he allows to remain in his life and thus loses his hold on God. According to the apostle Peter, "...of whom a man is overcome, of the same is he brought in bondage" (2 Peter 2:19). "Sad indeed is the condition" Ellen G. White comments, "of those who, becoming weary of the way, allow the enemy of souls to rob them of the Christian graces that have been developing in their hearts and lives."[4]

The main things that hinder the thorny-ground hearer are cherished sins and worldly ambitions.

Cherished Sins

There are few Christians who believe that every thorn (evil practice) must be uprooted from their lives. Many enjoy spiritual growth, but when brought to certain points where they are required to give up some evil practice, they draw back.

According to Ellen G. White,

"God leads his people on, step by step. He brings them into positions which are calculated to reveal the motives of the heart. Some endure at one point, but fall off at the next. At every advance step the heart is tested, and tried a little closer . . . . All who become connected with the cause of God will have opportunity to know what is in their hearts. If they prize anything higher than the truth, their hearts are not prepared to receive Jesus, and he is consequently shut out. If individuals, when tested, refuse to sacrifice their idols, and overcome selfishness, pride, and evil passions, it will be said of them as of Ephraim of old, They are joined to their idols, let them alone; and the Spirit of God will leave them with their sinful traits unsubdued, to the control of evil angels."[5]

"How few are aware that they have darling idols" she says, "that they have cherished sins! God sees these sins to which you may be blinded, and He works with His pruning knife to strike deep and separate these cherished sins from you. You all want to choose for yourselves the process of purification. How hard it is for you to submit to the crucifixion of self; but when the work is all submitted to God, to Him who knows our weakness and our sinfulness, He takes the very best way to bring about the desired results."[6]

The word of God cannot bear fruit in a heart that cherishes any known sin. Yes, God works with us step-by-step to remove sin from our lives. But, when He brings to our view any evil practice, we must put it away. According to Jesus, "If I had not come and spoken unto them, they had not had sin: but now they have no cloak for their sin" (John 15:22).

According to Matilda Andross, ". . . . the most obscure known sin hidden in the heart of any Christian will hinder him from living the life that counts. The terrible thing about little pet sins is that they do not stay little; they are bound to grow and ruin the life."[7]

Also, Ellen White comments, "Even one wrong trait of character, one sinful desire, persistently cherished, will eventually neutralize all the power of the gospel. Every sinful indulgence strengthens the soul's aversion to God."[8]

The principles of God's word are totally opposite to sin and selfishness. Therefore, if our lives are to be entirely built on God's word, every trace of sin must be removed for the word to bear fruit in our lives. "...let us lay aside every weight, and the sin which doth so easily beset us," Paul comments, "and let us run with patience the race that is set before us, Looking unto Jesus the author and finisher of our faith; who for the joy that was set before him endured the cross, despising the shame, and is set down at the right hand of the throne of God" (Hebrews 12:1, 2).

Those who are not careful to remove these thorns will eventually lose out on bearing fruit in the Christian life, despite how much growth they might experience.

Worldly ambitions

The thorns, according to the parable in Matthew 13, also represent "cares of this world" and the "deceitfulness of riches". This represents the experience of Christians who desire to have the best in the world and the best of the Christian life at the same time. This is a Christian who is too 'busy' for spiritual things.

Love for the world or love for money is a thorn that truly will (if cherished) grow up to choke the word in one's life. That is why the word of God counsels, "Love not the world, neither the things that are in the world. If any man love the world, the love of the Father is not in him" (1 John 2:15). "...godliness with contentment is great gain . . . . and having food and raiment let us be therewith content. But they that will be rich fall into temptation and a snare, and into many foolish and hurtful lusts, which drown men in destruction and perdition. For the love of money is the root of all evil: which while some coveted after, they have erred from the faith, and pierced themselves through with many sorrows" (1

Timothy 6:6, 8–10).

Jesus knew that it would be an impossible task for us to carry the burdens of this life on our own and pursue salvation at the same time; that is why He counsels us to put God first in our lives (see Matthew 6:24-34). "Therefore take no thought, saying, What shall we eat? or, What shall we drink? or, Wherewithal shall we be clothed? (For after all these things do the Gentiles seek:) for your heavenly Father knoweth that ye have need of all these things. But seek ye first the kingdom of God, and his righteousness; and all these things shall be added unto you" (Matthew 6:31-33). The management of our lives, securing a stable financial future for ourselves and children are concerns that every human being faces or must face at some point. These cares have the potential to absorb our attention; keep us busy all our lives. Nothing is wrong with being concerned about these things, for the Lord expects us to take care of our families. The problem is that some people seem to think that these concerns are so important and there is so much at stake that they cannot trust themselves in God's hands completely. They feel that they need to 'establish themselves'--removing all possibility of failure in this life before they can trust God completely. These are the ones who allow the "cares of this life" to choke the word, and thus bear no fruit for the glory of God. Also, those whose attention is absorbed with the 'cares of this life' are the ones who are usually led astray by the 'deceitfulness of riches.'

---

[1] Ellen G. White, *The Ministry of Healing*, 179.

[2] Ellen G. White, *Gospel Workers*, 254

[3] James Cres, *You Can Keep Them If You Care* (Silver Spring, Maryland: General Conference of Seventh-day Adventists, 2000), 27.

[4] Ellen G. White, *Acts of the Apostles*, 532-533.

[5] Ellen G. White, "Sanctification", *Review and Herald*, 1951 & 2014, 510.

[6] Ellen G. White, *Testimonies for the Church Volume 3* (EGW Writings

Online: Ellen G. White Estate, Inc, 1875), 543.

[7] Matilda Andross, *Alone With God* (Mountain View: Pacific Press Publishing Association, 1929 & 1961), 62.

[8] Ellen G. White, *Steps to Christ*, 34.

Conclusion

The Christian experience is a life of constant conflict against the forces of darkness; against self and sin. We must keep this battle up every day. Therefore, we should not use today's victory as an indication that we do not have to be so vigilant tomorrow. "Those who have felt the sanctifying power of the Holy Spirit and have tasted of the good life to come, should not think that they are sinless; that they have reached the highest state of perfection, and are beyond the reach of temptation."[1] Paul also warns, "Wherefore let him that thinketh he standeth take heed lest he fall" (1 Corinthians 10:12). "Examine yourselves, whether ye be in the faith; prove your own selves. Know ye not your own selves, how that Jesus Christ is in you, except ye be reprobates?" (2 Corinthians 13:5).

In the Christian life, it is not only important to gain victory over sin but to maintain that victory. It is because many do not understand this why they get discouraged and fail to continue their experience with the Lord when they realize that resisting temptation and the devil is something, they need to keep up every day; every moment. They get overwhelmed with the idea that they are called upon to live a righteous life, for so long, in such a sinful world. However, this (your hope of salvation) is part of the care that you are to cast upon the Lord, who cares so much for you. You need to have faith to believe, that though you are faced with temptation every day; old habits striving for the mastery, God "is able to keep you from falling, and to present you faultless before the presence of his glory with exceeding joy," (Jude 1:24). Your responsibility is to abide in Christ all the time, as the branch is connected to the vine, and He will cause you to bear the fruit that will bring glory to God (Psalm 1).

For some Christians, the problem is not knowing the "right" things to do; the problem is distraction. We know that for us to grow spiritually, we need to read our Bible, pray, go to church, obey the Holy Spirit and exercise faith. However, sometimes we get distracted by so many seemingly important things that we forget to do the things that are most important (Luke 10:38-42).

In addition to that, when we get distracted, Satan leads us into sin and by the time we get back on track, we begin to question whether doing the "right" things can truly protect us from temptations. We begin to think that success in the Christian walk is so elusive that no one can truly have that success when the real problem is that we got distracted. Not that we failed to do the right thing (the things that contribute to our growth) but that we failed to keep doing them. We fail to guard against distractions.

This is my word of encouragement to you dear reader. That you will not only understand what it takes to grow spiritually but that you will do them and keep on doing them. Let God take care of the miracle of growth. Just keep your eyes on the horizon. Keep your eyes on the only constant in this world—that is Jesus Christ, the Son of God. "Being confident of this very thing, that he which hath begun a good work in you will perform *it* until the day of Jesus Christ:" (Philippians 1:6).

---

[1] Ellen G. White, "Lowliness and Godly Sorrow". *Signs of the Times*, 1834.

About the Author

Damian Chambers is an ordained Pastor of the Seventh-day Adventist church. He has served the Central Jamaica Conference (CJC) as Pastor and Conference Director for over ten years. He is passionate about sharing the gospel using technology, writing and preaching. He is the author of the *Basic Bible Doctrines Bible Study Guides*, and the *Special Study on the Righteousness of Christ (Study Guide)*, published by the Inter-American Division of Seventh-day Adventists. He hosted two devotional radio programmes and one lifestyle interview programme on behalf of CJC for a combined four years.

Pastor Chambers holds a Master of Arts Degree in Pastoral Theology from the Inter-American Division Theological Seminary (IATS). He is also pursuing a Master of Science in Information Systems (MIS) from the Northern Caribbean University.

He is married to Roxanne Mckoy, a teacher by profession. They have two children, Jaheem Ricardo, and Janae Avielle.

In his leisure time, Pastor Chambers also enjoys Lawn Tennis, Table Tennis, Computer Programming, Football, and Cricket.

Made in the USA
Middletown, DE
09 March 2025

72430630R00069